ALL
KINDS OF
Mothers

ALL
KINDS OF
Mothers

Thoughts and Essays
by Women for Women

DESERET
BOOK

Salt Lake City, Utah

Interior images and endsheets: INGARA/Shutterstock.com

Library of Congress Cataloging-in-Publication Data

(CIP data on file)
ISBN 978-1-62972-747-9

Printed in China
Four Colour Print Group, Nansha, China

10 9 8 7 6 5 4 3 2 1

CONTENTS

Life's Little Lessons

One of the truths about motherhood we all discover is that we can positively dislike our children when we are jolted out of sleep to go tend to them, and another is that once we get to their bedside we can be bowled over by the *surge of love* we feel for the small, soft, hopelessly dependent human beings nuzzling against our warm and sleepy bodies. In those moments we learn the lesson the Lord means us to learn about love and service: the deeper the space we hollow out by unselfish service to others, the greater the area available to be filled with the love that is our mortal link with divinity.

BEPPIE HARRISON

SLOW-RIPENING FRUITS

Emily Watts

I am at the grocery store with my three-year-old daughter. She has the pint-sized grocery cart and is pushing it along beside me with my regular-sized cart. We are quite a picture, the two of us shopping together, me initiating my little girl into the mysteries of the grocery world. I can see it in the approving expressions of the shoppers passing us in Aisle 7: "Isn't that darling? What a lovely child. What a good mother."

Then we turn into Aisle 8, which is where the Oreos reside, right at the three-year-old's eye level. She chooses a package of cookies from the shelf and puts them in her cart. I pluck them out of the cart and return them to the shelf with a cheery if somewhat terse, "Not today, sweetheart. We're not going to buy those cookies today."

Well, perdition hath no fury like a three-year-old deprived of her Oreos, and she immediately flings herself to the ground and begins screaming. And I can see it in the disgusted expressions of the shoppers passing us in Aisle 8: "What a brat! Why doesn't her mother control her? Why would anyone bring a child like that out in public?"

Well, which is it? Angel child, or demon spawn? Am I a good mom or a bad mom? All too often, people will form that judgment depending on the moment in which they catch me at my mothering.

I want to grab the tantrum observers as they pass by and tell them that *this never works.* I never buy Oreos under coercion. I am a sensible, intelligent mother, with appropriate boundaries. But they have made their judgments based on what they see. Appearances. They can indeed be deceiving.

Here's a challenge, though: Don't the scriptures say, "By their fruits ye shall know them" (see Matthew 7:17; 3 Nephi 14:16)? They do. What they forget to remind us is that sometimes fruit takes a long time to ripen.

Think about this. Have you ever bitten into a fruit that's not ripe—a hard strawberry or a green melon or something like that? It's gross. All you really want to do is spit it out. If you were judging the fruit *based on that appearance at that time,* you might think the fruit was not good. But if you waited until the fruit was ripe and then tried it, you would see how delicious it could be.

An important thing to understand about raising children is that children are the slowest-ripening fruit there is.

Those precious fruits of our mothering take a long time to mature, and what's more, they all ripen at

4

different rates. So it's unproductive and even dangerous to base our feelings of mothering confidence on where the fruit is at any given time.

I went on a quest to try to understand better the truth that Heavenly Father is not just capable of helping me in my difficulties but willing and anxious to do so. I went to the heading *Trust* in the Topical Guide and found some wonderful scriptures that have helped me see things a little more clearly. The first one that I want to share with you is Psalm 27:14, which says: "Wait on the Lord: be of good courage, and he shall strengthen thine heart: wait, I say, on the Lord." This is not my favorite scripture because I have never been a very good waiter. It is not easy for me to have the courage it takes all along the way to wait for that child-fruit to ripen.

But waiting ultimately yields its rewards, little glimmers now and then that strengthen our hearts and give us hope that the fruit is coming along. That little girl who came to the grocery store with me occasionally (when I couldn't avoid it) is a good example of this. She has always had the blessing and the curse of knowing her own mind. The back of her bedroom door still bears the scars of where she used to kick it when she was in time out, learning to behave herself a little better. She wouldn't ever try to come out, but she would lie on her back on the floor and just kick the door.

That fruit takes a long time to ripen. It takes a

lot of faith, and a lot of spiritual insight and divine encouragement, to see it as it's really going to be. In the end, in order to
have the patience we need, we have to remember how fruit ripens.
Consider that we plant it, and we nurture it, and we water it, and
we do what we can, but the ripening of that fruit is mostly up to
the sun. It's the same with the fruit of our children. Ultimately,
their maturing depends largely on the Son. We have to trust
Him.

By our fruits we will be known. But not now. Not yet. We
need to give ourselves time, and give our children time.

One last thought regarding this principle occurred to me
when I was pondering it one day: What if the fruit of my parenting isn't my children at all? What if the fruit of me being a mom
is who *I* am becoming as a result of being that parent?

That thought changes the whole picture. I start to realize that
the children who are the hardest are very often the ones who are
making *me* the most of who I need to be. The problem children
(and they're all problem children at some point, I think) are the
ones who drive me to the arms of the Savior. They're the ones
whose challenges put me on my knees to ask their Father, "Thou
who lovest this child more than I do, wilt Thou help me understand what I need to do to bring him back to Thee?"

The fruit of my life is me, and most of what I know about
believing all things and hoping all things and enduring
all things (see 1 Corinthians 13:7), I have learned as a

result of being a mom. To me, the most interesting thing about that is that I have friends who would say that everything they know about believing and hoping and enduring has come to them because they haven't yet had a chance to be a mom. Isn't it amazing how Heavenly Father takes the circumstances of our mortality and uses them to mold us and make us who we need to be to return to Him?

There's much in life that isn't instant and isn't fast. Mothers don't sign up for an easy plan to have a baby in a few weeks. It's almost always around nine months—longer for elephants, shorter for guinea pigs. Skills and relationships and testimony and character traits—there are a lot of things that take time. For the most part, the things in our life that matter the most will have to be attended to. We will have to budget some time—make and take some time—for them. It's a process, sometimes a lifelong process. Enoch and his city were taken up "in process of time" (Moses 7:21).

One of our challenges is to figure out which are the *most important* things in our life—where we should be putting our time and our energy and our other resources—right now, in this season of our lives.

MARY ELLEN EDMUNDS

WHY WE ARE TAKING THE FUN OUT OF LIFE

Brooke Romney

My children have a problem. They think the purpose of life is to have fun. It was especially evident when their prayers included, "Help us to have a fun day tomorrow and a fun day the day after that." That little phrase hit me hard. Is our family so out of touch with others' needs and so removed from thanking the Lord that the only place we need God to intervene is to guarantee our fun? Where had we gone wrong?

After some serious self-reflection, I realized that we've been creating these fun-fed children. As they leave our car, we smile, wave, and shout, "Have fun!" After they return home from somewhere (school, practice, play date, church), the question is usually "Did you have fun?" and if they didn't, there is often a decent amount of concern about what might be wrong and how we can remedy this un-fun problem.

Not only that, but we live in a culture full of cheap thrills and expensive entertainment that everyone feels like he or she *must* be a part of. You don't take an annual trip to Disneyland?

Your poor kids! You aren't going to spend the day at a trampoline park? Bummer! Your kids don't have iPhones or iTouches yet? So sad! You aren't going away for the three-day weekend? What *will* you do at home?

Fun is a drug. Take a little and you want more. Take enough and it no longer satisfies. You need bigger, better, more expensive activities to fill you up. The simple moments are no longer satisfactory, and the big events don't seem all that big anymore. Fun is a junk food diet that leaves you giddy for a moment, then hollow and wanting more.

Kids learn it from somewhere: media, friends and, yes, parents too. Our culture worships leisure, entertainment, and fun. As parents, we have forgotten how to have a good time with our kids without paying someone to fabricate it for us. We have forgotten that the most fulfilling and closest relationships are not the ones based on constant fun together but ones where we have worked, laughed, loved, and struggled together. I don't want a cotton candy relationship with my kids. I want something substantial and real.

As I read biographies and listen to interviews about successful people who have changed the world, there seems to be a common thread in what they learned as children and adolescents: hard work. It doesn't matter which country they come from, their socioeconomic status, their gender, their beauty or lack of it. They succeed by working hard at something, for something or to merely survive, and these lessons almost always started at home.

So this year we are turning over a new leaf in our home. We are still huge advocates of enjoying life, seeing the positive, and taking it all in. We want to travel with our kids and show them the wonders of nature and different cultures. We love to play sports, take walks, visit the theater, attend concerts, hike, play games, swim, watch movies, and just be together.

But this year we will work hard together too. We will create memories and strengthen relationships as we accomplish difficult things together. We will hold our boys accountable for their efforts in our family, in school, in sports, in music, in hobbies, and in their church duties. We will no longer ask our kids if they had fun because, frankly, we don't care. They can choose to make every experience fun if they want to. It's up to them and absolutely possible. But we will no longer worry about creating fun for them or shielding them from hardships, unpleasantness or, heaven forbid, boredom. We want them to reap more than fun from this existence. We want them to be fulfilled. We want them to reach their potential. We want them to be excellent.

We will change our focus and ask one of these questions:

> "Did you learn something?"
> "Did you feel productive?"
> "Did you work hard?"

"Did you try your best?"
"Were you a good friend?"
"Did you try something new?"
"Did you push yourself?"
"Did you make someone's day better?"
"Did you add value?"
"Did you create something?"
"Did you grow?"
"Did you discover something?"
"Did you change the world today, even in a small way?"

When you can answer yes to any of those questions, that's when life gets really fun.

A young mother with five small children was busy at the kitchen counter fixing dinner. Her young son Tommy came running in and said, "Mom, Mom."

"Yes," she responded, as she continued working at the counter.

"Mom," he implored, "listen to me."

"I'm listening," she replied as she continued working.

"No," Tommy said. *"listen with your face!"*

MARILYN JEPPSON CHOULES

BETTER THAN PRIME

Jaroldeen Edwards

For years and years I had not even thought of the concept of a prime of life. My life had been so full of meaningful challenges, staggering amounts of work, living, complex relationships, and a growing focus and awareness of eternal goals that my young, simplistic view of an ultimate ideal mold into which I would eventually fit had long since lost any validity in my life. As a matter of fact, the best thing I had discovered in adult life was that I get to choose my own patterns, to put first the things that matter the most to me and to my family. Yet I had to stop and wonder how much of my sense of self and my list of priorities had been affected through the years by the expectations of society and a preconceived notion of the things that would spell success in the eyes of others.

My wonderful conclusion on that long-ago night, as I put my children to bed, kissed them goodnight, and looked at my rumpled, bumbling house full of things to do—some of which I loved doing and some of which I would procrastinate as long as

I decently could—was that I had not missed my prime at all. Oh yes, I had missed that prime pictured in the magazines; I would never be young and svelte, with coordinated towels, a perpetually clean refrigerator, and coordinated children. But I had not missed my prime—my own personal, wonderful, wouldn't-change-it-for-the-world prime. I had been living it every day all through the years.

To anyone else my life probably just looked noisy, confusing, disorganized, untidy, and improbable, but the point is that no one else gets to put the value on our life—no one but Heavenly Father and ourselves. To me all the years, even the hard ones, had been prime. Better than prime: choice.

I have chosen this life; it does not master me, I master it. I am not its victim, I am its recipient. And if there are times when I wistfully read a university catalogue, or wish that I could run instead of pushing a stroller and observing each leaf and stone, or get tired of the litany of "no's" and "do this's," those times are not frequent and they just serve to confirm that life is a banquet, and, even when filled, we hunger and thirst.

So it is that each day runs its course, filled with being, many things undone, many just begun. And thus to bed . . . and a continuing into the night.

THE BOOK OF MORMON
AT BREAKFAST

Neill Marriott

On an especially chaotic night, when dinner was not ready on time, many hungry children were prowling and growling around the kitchen. I saw the piled-up sink, noticed baby Davey crawling through cereal on an unswept floor, and heard sibling arguments flaring up. I wanted to cry. A Relief Society handout propped up by the kitchen window caught my eye, and I read:

"I feel certain that if, in our homes, parents will read from the Book of Mormon prayerfully and regularly, both by themselves and with their children, the spirit of that great book will come to permeate our homes and all who dwell therein. The spirit of reverence will increase; mutual respect and consideration for each other will grow. The spirit of contention will depart. Parents will counsel their children in greater love and wisdom. Children will be more responsive and submissive to the counsel of their parents. Righteousness will increase. Faith, hope, and charity—the pure love of Christ—will abound in our homes and lives, bringing in their wake peace, joy, and happiness" (Marion G. Romney, "The Book of Mormon," *Ensign,* May 1980).

At that moment, David arrived home from work. As he came through the back door into the kitchen, I held out the quote to him and said, in a voice shaking with emotion, "I want this!"

He approached rather cautiously, seeing that I was in high gear, took the paper from my hand, read, looked up, and said, "I do too."

Within the week David had unearthed the large, heavy Book of Mormon we had received as a wedding present. He placed it with some ceremony on the lazy Susan in the middle of our round dining table and announced that our family would begin reading the Book of Mormon every morning at breakfast. And read we did . . . at a snail's pace. In fact, the pace was so snaillike that *it took us seven years to read the Book of Mormon from cover to cover as a family.* I'm not proud of that three-verse-a-day speed, but we did it consistently, steadily, without fail. The second time through the scriptures, as the children were a little more grown up, we doubled our time. There was something powerful at work during breakfast. The hardback Book of Mormon collected remnants of breakfasts over the years—a gleam of syrup, a hardened spot of milk, a streak suggesting eggs. I love the historical record our stained book cover bears. It says, "I am loved, I am used, I am part of the fabric of this family—tattered, yes, but valued."

When our oldest son, Daniel, was a priest, he was asked to speak in a stake conference. I admit I hovered a bit and sweetly asked if I could be of any help, hoping I could polish his words so we would look as if we had raised an eloquent son. He would have none of it. When he began his talk with "It took my family seven years to read the Book of Mormon," I wanted to jump up and screech, "What do you expect with a family of thirteen at the breakfast table!" And then he put a match to the smoldering in my brain by adding, "And I don't really remember any specific verses that we read." But his next words rang out in gratitude: "What I do remember is that every single morning my dad reached for the Book of Mormon as we ate. And somehow I knew in my little-boy heart that this book was really important to my dad. Now it is important to me." I cried. There it was. Consistent daily family scripture reading, no matter how slow, is an undeniable witness of faith in the word of God.

Mothers Before

THE MOTHER OF ALL LIVING

Beverly Campbell

Who is this woman, the Mother of All Living, this Eve, who with Adam, the mighty premortal Michael, Ancient of Days, aided the Creator as this world was organized?

Why do we find her persona imprinted on virtually all cultures, all societies, and all religions? Why have these selfsame religions, societies, and cultures used her story to determine appropriate activities for women, to justify ecclesiastical positioning, and to extend or withdraw privileges and legal access to families, properties, and position?

What is her import that God would design a genetic fingerprint, a marker, whereby all children who have ever been or who will ever be born on this earth can be linked through their mothers to that first mother, Eve?

How could the actions of this righteous, grand, and noble daughter of our Heavenly Father have been so misunderstood? How could her ultimate gift to humankind—mortal life itself—have been overlooked?

With a soul hungering for truth and light as a body hungers for food, I began my search. Drawing on research shaped by the words our prophets have used to describe this first of all women, I wrote:

"Eve, first woman of earthly creation, companion of Adam and mother and matriarch of the human race, is honored by Latter-day Saints as one of the most important, righteous, and heroic of all the human family. Eve's supreme gift to mankind, the opportunity of life on this earth, resulted from her choice to become mortal."

Eve was at Michael's side before the foundations of the earth were set in place. Further, Eve's role was vital, for she was actively engaged in the planning and preparations that would shape our sphere. Eve was not merely a player on the stage after the Creation. As the leaders of the Church have taught, she was one of those "taking the materials and making the earth" (see Abraham 4). Certainly many of us were also privileged to participate.

God spoke to Eve of what she would experience as she embraced her destiny to be "the mother of all living" (Moses 4:26) as she and Adam complied with God's commandment to multiply and replenish the earth. These teachings were surely meant as instruction for Eve's daughters, who would follow after her. They are preserved in scripture.

Discernment, the ability to see beyond the

literal to the divine essential, has ever been God's gift to women. Since Eve, women have faced the challenge of ambiguous choices that carry with them holy, life-altering consequences. On the correct resolution of these ambiguities hangs the future of generations, the civilizing of society, the basic dignity of the human race, and mortal life itself. Daily, women must make decisions based on things not seen or even known clearly. Often these decisions require great leaps of faith. Frequently these decisions must be based on what serves the greater good for the greatest number. Often such decisions require women to set aside their own well-being in favor of another's. The very process of bearing children illustrates this truth dramatically. It is a source of strength and comfort to many women to know that inherent in their divine nature is this innate ability to be in tune with God's purposes.

Even more awe-inspiring is the knowledge that the Lord has such abiding faith in women's judgment and wisdom. By His very actions, He has shown women that He wants them to claim and properly act on this gift. Women are surely beloved of the Lord for Him to have placed them in such a position. As He relies on women to embrace the greater law, to bow to the greater commandment, He affirms their intellect, their integrity, and their righteousness.

MARY, THE MOTHER OF JESUS

Camille Fronk Olson

Fewer than ten days in the life of Mary, the mother of Jesus, are revealed in scripture, but all generations since her lifetime have been taught about her and have called her blessed. She was the mother of the Son of God—a loving mother during very challenging times. And she was an exemplary disciple of Jesus Christ, an inspired witness of God's gracious favor, and a guardian of remarkable truths. Unique among women in all of scripture, Mary is never portrayed in a negative light but is universally reverenced. Every mention of her signals purity, goodness, and discipleship.

We need not worship Mary to appreciate her contribution to God's work on earth. Her humble response to the angel's announcement of her role in the coming of the Son of God, "Be it unto me according to thy word," may qualify her as a pioneer Christian of the New Testament era, but it does not necessarily mean that she responded this way to anyone but God. Her realization that "all generations shall call me blessed" did not mandate her widespread worship but reflected her own sense of awe at the power of God, "for with God nothing shall be impossible" (Luke 1:38, 48, 37). Mary's conviction of God's reality and power deserves our admiration and emulation.

Watching her child grow from a helpless infant into a spiritually strong and exceptionally wise young man must have given Mary daily cause to marvel. She would have watched his physical growth much as other parents do, considering it occurred at a normal pace. But his spiritual and intellectual growth must have been astounding, quickly exceeding what she could teach him. The Joseph Smith Translation indicates that "he spake not as other men, neither could he be taught" (JST, Matthew 3:25). How often Mary must have felt inadequate, humbled, and also profoundly blessed to be this gifted child's mother. No doubt her own commitment to diligence in God's service was enhanced through observations of her completely and strikingly diligent Son.

As Jesus continued to increase "in wisdom and stature, and in favour with God and man," his mother was the one most likely to notice (Luke 2:52). Wisely, she "kept all these sayings in her heart" (Luke 2:51). Instinctively, she seemed to recognize that the answers to her questions would not come by broadcasting her observations to those around her or by complaining of her unique challenges to her neighbors. Instead, she pondered what she had been given and prepared herself to gain additional insights that would eventually lead her to understanding. Like her Son, she was gaining that understanding line upon line, grace by grace.

LOVE AND WARM TOWELS

Carolyn Rasmus

My mother lived to be ninety-four. We'd had a lot of differences over the years. There is just something sometimes about a mother and a daughter that doesn't quite click, especially when both are very strong-willed women. But in her later years, I went home to help take care of her. My father had passed away, and she was living with her sister, who was just two years younger.

We had help that came in, but one day I said, "Why don't I just give you a bath?" And so I did. I was a little awkward at first, and she was a little awkward at first. But we got past that, and I remembered that when I was growing up, one of the things my mother would do for me when I took a bath was to hang the towels on the radiator so that they would be warm, and then when she'd hear me get out of the bathtub, she would slip the towel in to me, and it would be all nice and warm. I loved that.

So as we were finishing Mom's bath, I quickly took three towels and ran and put them in the dryer. I helped her get out of the bathtub and sit down on the toilet, and then I ran and got those three hot towels and wrapped her up in them. I looked at her, and she had tears running down her face. She said: "*I* should be taking care of *you*. How did you remember about the towels?"

Well, it was one of those moments when I think all of the hurt and all of the pain went away. I think it was one of those "tender mercies" when the Lord intervened and our hearts were brought together.

A DISARMING HUMOR

Kathleen H. Walker

I always assumed that motherhood would be easy. As the oldest child, I had watched Mother welcome each subsequent new baby into our family. It appeared to me to be an occasion that was unequaled in this life. Mother's ease with her children led me to believe that all of motherhood was joy, bliss, and complete satisfaction. She would tell me that the experience of childbirth was akin to dipping into heaven for a brief moment and returning with this blessed new infant. She said that with each new baby came a bundle of love so love never ran thin. She told me that the greatest joys in life were those associated with your children. It appeared to be all true.

When our youngest sister was born, I was ecstatic. I would jump off the school bus each school afternoon and run all the way home, so anxious was I to get home to the new baby. I held her and dressed her and fed her and bathed her. I took her for walks, and when she fussed I handed her to Mother. I agreed with Mother. Having a baby of your own would be the best!

Is it any wonder, then, that my intense hunger for my own baby started immediately after I was married? I would often imagine my day with a baby in it. I would see myself holding a baby, dressing a baby, cooing to a baby, loving a baby. I could hardly wait till my dream came true. But, as that blessed state of impending motherhood descended upon me, I found myself sick! Very sick! I couldn't eat or even smell anything that resembled food. I couldn't wake up, and slept night and day. My head was continually in a fog. This was not the way I had pictured it.

The night this first little infant was born didn't exactly feel like a trip to heaven. It was long, miserable, and something I vowed I would never repeat. When she finally arrived, I thought the hard part was over and from this moment forward, the bliss part of motherhood would begin.

Wrong. I took the baby home, thinking the routine of my life would quickly be resumed. My fantasies of dressing her in bows and lace were just around the corner. She was so cute—in fact, she was beautiful. This was going to be great after all.

But I was ill prepared for what I faced. This tiny little six-pound bundle instantly took total control of my life. She determined when I could sleep, when I could eat, when I could shower, clean my house, do my laundry, where and if I could go anyplace. Not only that, everything I did was done in a state of complete fatigue. About six weeks into this I looked around one day and knew that this was not the life

I planned. And suddenly I desperately wanted out. Motherhood was not all it was cracked up to be. I wanted my old life back. I could not bear the thought of living the rest of my life out of control, in a completely fatigued state. In a flood of tears I dialed my mother.

"I've had it!" I cried to my mother. "I'm not cut out to be a mother! I can't do this the rest of my life. This child has taken over. I'm not even a person anymore. I want my old life back!"

She listened quietly as I unloaded for several tearful minutes. Then, quite unexpectedly, she started to laugh. "Well, guess what, dear," she said through her laughter. "It's too late!"

Her upbeat, jovial response disarmed me. I was completely taken aback. She had managed with that simple, light quip to bring me back to earth. The fact that she found my tragic situation funny suddenly allowed me to step outside myself and see how pathetic I looked. It was a comical sight. And somehow her laughter let me know that she knew what this was like and that it wouldn't last forever.

On so many occasions since then, Mother's disarming humor has put things into perspective. She takes life seriously, but she doesn't take herself seriously.

What a gift!

A MOTHER'S EXAMPLE

Mary Holland McCann

As we study Mary and observe her characteristics, it is not hard to imagine why Heavenly Father would have chosen her to be the mother of the Son of God. The faith, submission, and reverence we see in her are also characteristics the Savior manifests. For example, her courage to continually choose faith over fear is an attribute we see in Jesus throughout His entire life. In fact, we do not ever encounter the word *fear* or any synonym for it in any of the Savior's most difficult moments. He felt pain, anguish, loss, and sorrow, but we do not ever read of Him exhibiting fear. Because He was mortal and experienced "pains and afflictions and temptations of *every* kind" (Alma 7:11; emphasis added), we assume He was not immune to this emotion, yet He never seemed to be found caught up in it. Perhaps that is simply because His faith was always too great. We cannot know, but what we do know is that from the time of His conception, His mother chose faith over fear. There can be no doubt that Jesus would have learned this principle at her knee.

Similarly, Mary's submission and desire to glorify God are also traits we see in the Savior's life over and over again. He submitted to the will of the Father and directed all glory to Him in every thought and deed. This was nowhere more evident than when He was suffering the unbearable pain and agony of Gethsemane. During this, the most lonely and agonizing moment of His mortal life, He cried for relief but then meekly prayed, "Not my will, but thine, be done" (Luke 22:42). In this expression of perfect submission, one can hear an echo of Mary's words thirty-three years earlier as she uttered, "Behold the handmaid of the Lord; be it unto me according to thy word" (Luke 1:38). Knowing that the Savior would live a life of submission, it is little wonder that Heavenly Father chose Mary to help teach and guide Him.

As with her faith and submission, Mary's reverence for sacred things was a very visible trait in the Savior's life. Even during His most public ministry, He made time to fast and pray and commune with His Father alone (see Luke 5:16; 6:12). Those were experiences He did not share. In fact, He admonished us to be careful that we "give not that which is holy unto the dogs, neither cast ye your pearls before swine, lest they trample them under their feet" (Matthew 7:6). The scriptures even attest to numerous miracles the Savior performed that were followed by His request that those who witnessed these miracles were to "tell no man" (Matthew 8:4). Even the Savior of the world, who came to save souls in part through His miracles, was selective about what to share and what to keep sacred—something He surely learned, at least to some extent, from His mother.

What I hope we, as mothers, learn from Mary and Jesus is that we need to *be* the kind of people God wants our children to become. It is far less important to plan the perfect family home evening or buy all the copies of the scripture videos for your children to watch than it is to *be* what it is you are trying to teach them.

SHE DID THIS FOR ME

Virginia U. Jensen

We live in a world filled with rocks of all sizes. It was created that way by divine design, as a proving ground for our faith and a vital step in our eternal progression. One of the great tasks of our mortal life is to learn that, through the grace and mercy of Jesus Christ, we can climb every rock, or overcome every challenge, that we encounter.

Some of the rocks in our lives are self-chosen. For example, most mothers would admit that their children can be both their greatest blessing and their greatest trial. Many of the things mothers slog through daily—fixing meals, doing laundry, running the perpetual carpool, helping with homework, sitting up late at night with sick babies or heartsick teenagers—are natural outgrowths of the choice to have children. It's not always convenient to be a mom, and it's certainly not always easy. Yet we would make that choice again if we were starting from scratch,

rocky though it may be at times. Sometimes it helps to remind ourselves that we really wanted those children.

I remember when I was wheeled out of the delivery room after giving birth to my first child. I had two thoughts. The first was *Did anyone get the license number of the truck that just hit me?* The second was *Wow, my mother did this for me.* Suddenly I had an incredible increase in appreciation and love for my mother, and I realized I had a tremendous debt to repay her in love, respect, devotion, and service.

SHE'S WITH MY MOMMY

Calee Reed

For a few years I was a single, full-time mom living in my dad's basement. I was working two jobs—one in a doctor's office and the other as a singer-songwriter for Deseret Book. I had never dreamed that I'd get a divorce. Never anticipated living in my dad's basement in my thirties. There were so many times I wished I could call my mom and ask for her help or advice—but she died in 2011 after a brutal battle with colon cancer.

Fast forward to July of last year. All of my single-mom/ divorcee-dating-woes seemed to be coming to an end when I met and began dating the most wonderful man. He was funny, kind (*so* kind), and levelheaded. The only thing that gave me pause in falling immediately head over heels was the fact that he was a widower with four children. Having lost my own mom, and having struggled intensely with my dad's quick remarriage, I was hesitant to move past casual dating with him. I knew how insanely difficult it is to lose your mom, and my heart ached at the thought of causing more distress for his four babes, ages eight to two. Dating him also meant facing some of my deepest triggers with doubt and heartache—it reminded me that I had so many questions still about the way Mom had died and why it all had happened.

I had an experience a few weeks after we started dating, though, that helped me see pieces of beauty in losing my mom.

It happened one Sunday when we decided to go to church together for the first time. I was nervous. Going to church together is a big deal in my world—and we had all of the kids (he had four kids and I had Vi, five kids total), and I was half expecting it to go so horribly that we'd just break up and never speak again afterward.

About halfway through the service, one of the twin six-year-old boys was sitting next to me, nestled under my arm.

He looked up and whispered, "Do you know where my mommy is?"

My mama-heart wrenched inside of my chest as I said, "Yeah, buddy. She's in heaven."

We sat in silence for a moment.

"Do you know who she's with?" I whispered.

"Who?"

"*My* mommy," I said. He smiled.

The love that I felt as I looked down at that little boy was so overwhelming that I had to quickly wipe away the tears. The empathy from that shared heartbreak overwhelmed me; it felt like a hurricane. A massive, unquantifiable explosion of love for him.

I don't pretend to understand why God would take the mother of these four beautiful children home so early—just like I don't understand why He took my mom the way that He did. But as I sat there looking down into that little boy's face, the beauty and sacredness of being able to connect on that level with another precious child of God through shared grief amazed me.

That experience on our first Sunday at church together will remain a cherished one for me. I look forward to the next decade or so of sitting next to that same little boy in church because I now have the privilege of calling him my son.

I have seen the way that God has shaped me through my trials and heartaches over the course of my lifetime. I believe that that is God's true intention: to shape us, to perfect us, and to sanctify us through all the burdens and challenges that we face. I believe that our refining process can be beautiful, even when painful, if we will open our hearts to see it.

The Love of a Mother

SYMBOLS IN MOTHERHOOD

Wendy Ulrich

When we're trying to unpack a spiritual symbol, we can start by asking what the symbol reminds us of, or what it is like. When you think of baptism, the sacrament, or ordinances of the temple, ask yourself what they are like. Do any of these come to mind?

A midwife at the birth of a baby
A parent feeding a meal to a family
A parent washing and dressing a wound for a child
A bride changing her name when she marries
A mother dressing her daughter for her wedding
A grandparent greeting a family member after a long absence

I can't help but notice how common these events are in the lives of women. They are not all *exclusively* female experiences, to be sure, but they are certainly *common* female experiences, and if we want to understand the mighty spiritual realities underlying gospel ordinances, being a woman may help. Consider the symbol of baptism. How is this like our mortal birth? Of course, we don't remember being born, so we don't have a lot of personal experience to draw on there. So let's go to the other side of the birth experience. What is birth like for a mother? For a midwife? Who is the mother and midwife of our new birth? The Savior.

When I was pregnant with our first child, my husband Dave gave me a beautiful priesthood blessing. In it, he unexpectedly promised me that during this pregnancy I would gain special insight into the Atonement of Jesus Christ. Excited, I began studying scriptures about the Atonement in search of this insight. Nothing particular jumped out. I prayed fervently for help in knowing how to secure this blessing. *Nada.* I read a book about the Atonement. Interesting, but nothing new. Pregnancy rolled on. I didn't get any special insight into Christ's Atonement. I just got increasingly tired and uncomfortable.

And then I went into labor. I began to suffer. Despite the intellectual understanding I had from books about what labor and delivery would involve and how to relax and breathe my way through it, this was a whole new ballgame. I felt completely unprepared. I wondered how I would survive this process that took over my body. I bled. I cried out. I prayed. I longed for someone to help me, or at least to stay with me while I endured. I remember falling to my knees and crawling on the floor with the pain of transition. During delivery I broke out in a rash of little red dots across my face and torso from the pressure of pushing. A necessary sacrifice, one more painful than I had previously imagined, secured new life for someone I had not even met in this life. And I loved that person in ways I had never experienced before.

Oh. *That* kind of insight into the Atonement of Christ.

If we want to learn about baptism, our "new birth," we may get only as far as imagining a warm bath unless we think about what birth really is like for a woman in labor. Is there anything the Atonement of Christ is more "like" than labor, a woman's labor, bringing new life to an unborn child (see Isaiah 53:11)?

There is some kind of special *power* that
seems to leak from beyond the veil at the time
when mothers are the conduit from there,
bringing forth their newborns. It gets all over
mothers and gives them a *special vision*.

KATHLEEN "CASEY" NULL

PACKING UP A LIFE

Elaine S. Dalton

All my life I have been passionate about the role of motherhood. I feel and have always felt that I could impact the world more by being a good mother and raising a righteous, qualified family than through anything else I could do.

I believe that if a woman can manage an efficient, organized, Spirit-filled home, whether married with children or single, she can do almost anything. I believe it is in the home that we learn discipline, communication skills, interpersonal skills, negotiation skills, how to compromise, and how to multitask. It is in the home that we learn scheduling skills, management skills, public relations skills, budgeting, conscious consumerism, goal setting, and interpersonal relationship skills. It is in a home setting that we learn fairness, values, ethics, and long-range planning, and so many more things. And the Lord outlines the pattern to follow in Doctrine and Covenants 109: "That this house may be a house of prayer, a house of fasting, a house of faith, a house of glory and of God" (D&C 109:8).

We can never measure the extent of our influence as righteous women. A few years ago my daughter-in-law Annie went to her family home to pack its contents. Her mother had passed away just one month after Annie married our son Jess. She was heart-broken. She later told me how hard it had been. Her remark was, "How do you pack up a life and put its contents in little boxes and distribute it to whomever?"

My response was, "You don't. You only pack *things*. Life goes on in the evidence, and the evidence is *you*. It is your life well lived. It is your example. It is carrying on the things your mother taught you and honoring your heritage and legacy by making honorable and good choices. It is pressing forward. It is maintaining "a perfect brightness of hope" (2 Nephi 31:20). It is passing on all that your mother taught you. Her life is not in a box." It is really true—the lives of mothers and righteous, covenant-keeping women affect generations.

We are mothers whether we have children in our home or not. We can be mothers to others' children and nurture and warn and protect and love them, too. Who knows what our influence might do? I invite you to look around. Who needs you and your influence? Who needs your healing, nurturing touch? Who needs someone to understand them and to believe in them? Who needs to hear you say, "Everything will be all right," or "I just know you can do it," or "I love you"? If we really want to make a difference, it will happen as we mother our own children and those others who need us.

Common sense, woman's intuition, mother love—whatever it is called, each of us has a *reservoir* of good judgment and inspiration that is ours to help us in making those on-the-spot decisions or preventing impending disaster.

AFTON DAY

BUILDING A NEST

Virginia H. Pearce

A mother hummingbird builds a new home. She must create a place of physical safety and warmth, where she can give birth to, care for, and then launch her wee ones into the world.

Finding bits of fluff, soft plant matter, twigs, straw, and leaves, she weaves, pokes, and tamps them into shape. Adding spider webs to give the nest strength and flexibility, she works patiently, diligently. Back and forth, hither and yon, each nest is its own individual creation, made up of unique materials but perfectly, perfectly serviceable. This little cup will securely hold her tiny eggs as she seals the opening with her own warmth—her life force. Is this pure instinct? I think so.

Like our busy little friend, we mothers prepare for our babies. We instinctively want a home that can physically lock out intruders. One where we can be warm when winter storms rage. One with a roof to shelter us from scorching sun.

But you and I are more purposeful than a hummingbird. You see, we desire more than physical safety. We add to basic instinct a God-given desire for the spiritual safety of our loved ones. We want a place where we can teach them, watch them grow in confidence and skill. We want them to know how to build loving and satisfying relationships. We want them to be prepared to contribute to the world, to be strong in the face of evil and adversity, to make and keep sacred covenants, and to ultimately be prepared to go back to their eternal home. And we know that as we teach them, we will also learn and grow.

Yes, we want our homes to be "thin places" where we, and all those who enter, can experience God. What does that look like? Surely it doesn't mean a building with the finest appointments and workmanship. A place of complete order where people speak only in hushed tones, with light colored carpet and occasionally some soft organ music?

Wouldn't that be lovely! But in truth, our homes often resemble busy airports with people constantly coming and going. There seems to be an abundance of "stuff" that grows on every surface and spills onto floors. In these home-temples we laugh and cry together, experience anger and frustration as well as deep and spoken love. In our homes we sustain hurt and pain, make mistakes, learn, repent, forgive, change. Home is a refuge, but it is also a laboratory, a classroom. But in all this confusion we sense something grand. Isn't growing toward Godhood holy work? No wonder our homes are second only to temples in their sacredness.

PINT-SIZED PEOPLE

Zandra Vranes

I once heard Pastor T.D. Jakes say that there are pint-sized people and there are gallon-sized people. That when you're a gallon person, you can pour into a pint person and the relationship will be everything they need it to be because you have the capacity to fill them up. But a pint person could pour all they have into you, but it doesn't fill you up because you need a gallon. He said that we need to recognize that there are relationships in our lives where the person is truly giving us all they have, and no, it is not enough, it isn't everything we need. But it is all they have; they gave us everything they could.

As I've thought about his message throughout the years, that recognition has freed me to adjust my expectations regarding my life relationships, change my interactions or limit them when necessary, and above all extend forgiveness and grace. I've also come to believe that we aren't always one or the other, a pint or a gallon. There are portions of my life where I only have pint-sized capacity and capabilities, but gallon-sized responsibilities. And

I've had to admit that I've poured every last drop of myself into a bucket that I simply cannot fill on my own. There are times when I have been the gallon running around pouring into other's pints and watching them be restored through me, and I am left depleted with my gallon running dry. Sometimes you're the gallon with a steady flow pouring into a pint and you're drowning them because you have so much to give, but they can only hold so much; you can't pour a gallon into a pint.

As people of faith, our relationships can sometimes become our greatest anxiety. We worry about all the pouring and filling it takes to be with our loved ones, together, in the next life. I know that what we do in this life matters in the next, but I also know that what we don't do in this life matters there too. If we don't spend our time learning how to love each other on earth, will we even want to be with each other in heaven? There are days when "Families Can Be Together Forever" sounds more like a threat than a promise, and some of us are thinking, "They *can* be, but do they *have to be*?"

As I strive to keep my covenants, I've been prompted to be more aware of glimpses of what eternity can be instead of being anxious about whether my life or my family looks like a picture-perfect Church magazine or Proclamation family. When everyone isn't in the temple together, can you still see the moments that togetherness brought the temple to your home? One Sunday, as my mum poured into me, I realized that with love, simple homes can become sacred spaces. If we let them. It's not preaching or pestering—it's the moments like these that keep my eyes on eternity. A girl is never too old to sit between her mother's knees and have her comb her hair, to receive her love and allow her to give it in the ways she can give it best. There is no crown that adorns me better than the ones she has created upon my head, taught to her between her mother's knees, and rooted back through ancestors further than the eye can see. This is a glimpse of my eternity, for there is no kingdom I can strive for that doesn't have this.

Saints, do you see them in *your* life? Create the moments of eternity today that make an eternal family worth striving for tomorrow. Let that be our focus, and the Lord will work out our forever better than we could ever hope for.

YOU ARE THEIR PERFECT MOTHER

Whitney Permann

Last Valentine's Day I was feeling blue.

I saw the fun things my friends were doing with their kids—throwing Valentine's tea parties, making sugar cookies, and serving red-and-pink meals.

And I was wishing I was that kind of mom.

I don't craft, I'm not a great baker, and I've never hosted a tea party. But I wanted to make this particular Valentine's special, and I started to feel sad that my kids didn't have a cutesy, crafty mom.

On Valentine's night, after our plain, normal-colored dinner, we sat in the living room while my kids dug through their Valentine's loot (pointing out that I was *the* only mom that didn't attach candy to their valentines. See?).

But then something happened.

My husband spontaneously turned on some fun music. I jumped up and grabbed a kid off the couch, and we danced. Our living room quickly became a loud, crazy dance party. And everyone, from my husband down to the baby, was dancing. Suddenly, I realized what kind of mom I am.

I'm Crazy Dance Party Mom.

I can't frost a cookie to save my life, but I can crank up some music and party like I just don't care.

Because that's who I am.

It was then, in my living room, watching my kids swirl and laugh and dance around me, that I realized it: I am the best mom for my kids.

God gave them to *me*. He didn't give them to Crafty Mom. Or Tea Party Mom. Or Intricate-Hairstyle Mom. And He knows what He's doing.

I can picture Him saying, "Hmmmm. These five kids need a mom who can dance and be silly with them. I'll send them to Whitney. Wait . . . why is she trying to bake heart cookies and make homemade valentines? Oh, it's because she's trying to keep up with her neighbor. Ooooh. She just burned half the cookies and she's going to have to run to the store and get the last three boxes of generic dog and cat valentines on the shelf because hers didn't turn out. She's close to hysterics. And now she's yelling at her son because he dropped the milk jug while she was trying to update her Facebook status ('V-day fun with the kiddos!') I wish she would stick to what she does best. Which is dance parties."

Do you see?

God made *you* the mother of your children because He needs you to do "you" things with them.

That doesn't mean we can't try new things, or do things with our children that *they* enjoy. It simply means we can stop worrying that we aren't mothering our kids the way our friends are mothering theirs. There *is* a right way to mother *your* kids, and that's by capitalizing on your own God-given strengths. They're yours because they need what you have.

Do you love schedules? Your kids need a scheduler. Do you love sports? Your kids need an athlete. Do you love stories? Your kids need a storyteller.

They don't need any other kind of mom.

It's a truth I learned powerfully that Valentine's night. Our best mothering happens when we mother authentically—not when we're trying to do it like someone else.

So relax. Don't force it. Put your mom blinders on and focus only on what matters: your kids. God has given you specific tools and talents to raise them. And although you aren't perfect, you *are* their perfect mother.

Coming to earth, a newborn baby turns
a pristine page in his book of life.
His mother has the *first opportunity*
to affect its contents—establishing
continuity with the past, influencing
direction for the future.

BARBARA B. SMITH & SHIRLEY W. THOMAS

LIKE A LIONESS AT THE GATES OF THE HOME

Margaret D. Nadauld

How do you have a home where magic happens? I believe that it begins with a good woman—a mother—on high alert with one goal in mind: the well-being of her family and those within the sphere of her influence, a mother whose desire is to build and strengthen others. When you have had your hand on the pulse of your family for a lifetime you can usually diagnose the trouble and find a treatment for what ails.

Mothers have their children convinced that they see all and know all, especially when it comes to the well-being of their children. There really is something about a mother's watchful care that seems to give her an extra sense of alertness to dangers or evils on behalf of her children. Former Relief Society General President Julie B. Beck has encouraged mothers to be "like [a lioness] at the gate of the home."

What can we learn from a lion?

Picture with me a scene on the Nature Channel of a mother lion and her cubs. She senses that there are dangers lurking on every hand and that her babies are vulnerable and so she keeps a watchful eye. She watches as they romp and play and she knows that should she turn away for a time and get distracted, her cubs could be dinner for the nearest predator. And so she is a protector. As she works with her cubs, they gradually grow strong and confident and independent. And so she is a preparer. Mothers are like lionesses. They too protect and prepare.

The predators lurking after your precious children are well-known to you. Therefore you keep a vigilant eye on what goes on. Protect your family from birth with spiritual training. Teach them by your example and loving words to love the Lord, to worship Him, to follow Him. Show them how happy you are as you keep the commandments.

Prayer is a priceless protection. Teach your children to pray individually as they kneel by their bed.

A wise mother *prepares* her children. The lioness knows by instinct that the very survival of her young depends on the preparation she has provided. She is no-nonsense.

We tenderhearted mothers have to remind ourselves to purposefully prepare our children to be strong physically and emotionally, self-sufficient, and independent. We have to be careful so that our children aren't so pampered that they become too soft to do hard things. What a blessing it is to learn to work hard.

To you who are watchful mothers but have had disappointment with children, I want to say something:

No matter how vigilant a mother is, life is filled with opportunities for exercising agency. Choices abound and children are not immune from poor choices no matter how carefully you have taught and how perfectly watchful you are. When a child makes poor choices, then disappointment becomes your companion and weighs heavily on the heart of the faithful mother. Please, in the face of disappointment, don't leave your post. Be ever-ready by the gates of your home with love and sure knowledge that your efforts have not been in vain and some day and some time and some place you will see that by small and simple things are great things brought to pass as you see a miracle unfold in the life of a repentant loved one.

To mothers who may have times of doubt concerning the value of standing watch at your appointed post, like a lioness at the gates of the home, take courage! It is worth every effort, every pleading prayer, every personal sacrifice you make to labor valiantly and tirelessly in the vineyard of your home for the salvation of your children (see D&C 138:56). Please know that you are the one, now is the time, this is the place for every mother to have the courage to stand as one who protects and prepares her family. Bless your family with your love and your strength and one day, one day they will arise up and call you blessed. May you be blessed with encouragement and filled with peace as you go forward in your most valuable work.

Other Mothers

ARE WE NOT ALL MOTHERS?

Sheri Dew

When we understand the magnitude of motherhood, it becomes clear why prophets have been so protective of woman's most sacred and divinely appointed role. While we tend to equate motherhood solely with maternity and to, in effect, limit it to that definition, in the Lord's language the word *mother* has layers of meaning. Of all the words or titles they could have chosen to define her role and her essence, both God the Father and Adam called Eve "the mother of all living" (Moses 4:26)—and they did so before she ever bore a child. "And Adam called his wife's name Eve, because she was the mother of all living; for thus have I, the Lord God, called the first of all women, which are many" (Moses 4:26).

The Lord does nothing with a short-range view. Everything He does is for forever. Thus, like Eve, our motherhood began before we were born. Just as worthy men were foreordained to hold the priesthood in mortality (see Alma 13:2–4, 7–8), righteous women were endowed premortally with the privilege and responsibility of motherhood. Motherhood is more than bearing children, though it is certainly and definitely that. It is the essence of who we are as women. Motherhood defines our very identity, our divine stature and nature, and the unique traits, talents, and tendencies with which our Father endowed us.

Eve set the pattern. In addition to bearing children, she mothered all of mankind when she made the most courageous decision any woman has ever made and with Adam opened the way for us to progress. She set an example of womanhood for men to respect and women to follow, modeling the characteristics with which we as women have been endowed: heroic faith, a keen sensitivity to the Spirit, an abhorrence of evil, and complete selflessness. Like the Savior, "who for the joy that was set before him endured the cross" (Hebrews 12:2), Eve, for the joy of helping initiate the human family, endured the Fall. She loved us enough to help lead us.

All around us are those who need to be loved and led, nurtured and mentored. The spiritual rewards of mothering are available to all.

As daughters of our Heavenly Father, and as daughters of Eve, we are all mothers and we have always been mothers. And we each have the responsibility and the privilege to love and to help lead the rising generation. One of the single most significant responsibilities for a latter-day woman of God—regardless of her personal circumstances—is to help love and lead the younger generation. If we don't mentor them, no one will. If we don't show them there is joy in living as followers of Christ, where else can they possibly expect to see it!

Every woman of God, regardless of our individual circumstances, can mother someone—beginning of course with the children in our own homes and families, but extending far beyond. Every woman of God can show by word and by deed that the work of women in the Lord's kingdom is magnificent and holy. How far will we go to rescue a child or rally a teenager to righteousness? For when we save a young man or a young woman, we may save generations. I repeat: Every woman of God is a mother in Israel, and our calling is to help love and help lead the rising generation through the dangerous streets of mortality.

If we look with compassion on our own young ones and lead them toward *peace*, wherever we are with them can become a fruitful *haven*, a watered garden, whatever their current hard ground, weeds, and drought.

—FRANCINE R. BENNION

COMPARING SCARS

Laurel C. Day

I did not marry until the age of forty-one, and one of the ironies of my life is that I was given one deeply desired hope of my heart—marriage—a little too late to have the blessing of another: children of my own—a posterity. For different reasons, it is not in the cards for me. That fact has been the source of more hurt in this life than I can adequately express. You might say it is my biggest scar.

However, with this marriage came four stepsons (and two daughters-in-law), and now two adorable grandsons. I love these people. They have been gracious to let me into their lives, and I love what they have added to mine.

I would have never imagined I could love them as much as I love them and have desires for their happiness like I do. They are my family, and there are moments when I forget that I am the new person here. There are times when it truly feels like enough. And only God (and now perhaps my husband) knows what a miracle that is. How this new family situation seems to be filling in for a lifetime of wanting. That is a miracle!

Now, this is not to say that there are not moments that the reality of this particular scar still overcomes my little heart with sadness. When we were preparing to send boy #4 on his mission, someone said to me (and I know it was well intentioned but that didn't make it sting any less), "When you say goodbye, just know there will be fewer tears than there would be if you had raised him for all those years."

Why do we do that? Why do we compare scars? Who's to say my tears aren't any more deep and difficult than the woman who got to raise this boy? Conversely, I don't have the right to think my tears are any greater than hers.

But we compare scars when we say (or think) things like:

"Why is she so upset she can't have a third child? At least she has two!" Or, "I'm sorry you can't have children, but at least you're married." Or, "I'm sure it's hard her daughter is living a lifestyle that she doesn't agree with. But it's got to help that her son got married in the temple." Or, "Oh, you have MS? Well, at least it's not cancer!"

Our scars are our scars. If we thought life would be one way and it's not, there's a gap. And the difficulty of that gap is ours. And ours alone.

The morning we said goodbye to Mason, my tears (and holy cow there were a lot of them) might not have been tears of goodbye to a kid I had raised, but they were tears of goodbye for the kid I didn't get to. They were the tears for the three years that weren't nearly long enough and the tears for the ending of a life phase that never really happened. I found myself overcome with the emotion of all I had missed out on and the little time I'd had. And not just for this kid but for the houseful of children I'd wanted for as long as I can remember. Simply put, my heart felt cheated. It was one of those moments I'm not proud to admit occurred: that in the midst of a blessed life, I was focused on what I didn't have, jealous for what is not mine and sad for all I had missed.

In that moment, none of it was enough. I wasn't the bronze medalist thrilled to just be there at the airport; I was the girl with the silver watching all the other "regular families" having the "gold experience."

And no sooner did I admit to feeling all that when the Spirit, through my husband, said, "But aren't you glad we made the most of this time we had?"

Making the most of the time we have.

Finding comfort in what we've been given.

Seeing the *enough* in what we lack.

Being content with the years ahead and not looking at the shortage of the years behind.

There is something about that that I am convinced is the essence of life, the power of the Atonement, and the key to understanding the magnificent love of a watchful Father who compensates in His own way and in His own time every righteous desire of our heart.

I trust that. I believe that.

ANIMAL PANCAKES

Mary Cook

I became part of the Cook family as a stepmother over twenty-six years ago. My husband had been widowed and had a well-established family of four adult children and eight grandchildren under the age of eight. I remember well a particularly hard day in the early part of our marriage when my husband, Richard, said, "Mary, you have to understand that right now you're out of the Cook tent, and you may never be fully in." Well, I took that comment as a great challenge!

It was an overwhelming experience for all of us at first. Like most families, the Cooks had their traditions, their recipes, and their ways of doing things. So I went to where my heart felt most comfortable—the grandchildren. I had been an elementary school teacher, and children had always been easy to love. That first year of marriage had its challenges, but gradually, as I sought out the hearts of the grandchildren, the tent door started to crack open.

Since three of the four children lived out of state, we had large family gatherings at our home in Park City. The little ones were always the first to awaken, so I made an effort to make breakfast an "Event." As a child, my mother would make pancakes in the shape of a cat. I started with cats, then expanded my repertoire with requests such as: "Can you make me a giraffe?" "How about a Tyrannosaurus Rex?" I am not an artist, but I was pretty good at convincing little ones I could make anything! We would laugh and use our imaginations to determine what my mistakes were. (They still say Michael Jordan dunking a basketball was my greatest feat.) Breakfast and animal pancakes became a bonding experience for us.

Recently, I got a text from three of those little ones, now grown and attending BYU. "Hey, we're in Park City and it looks like it might snow. May we come over and stay?" As young coeds do, they arrived late that night, after we had gone to bed.

The next morning I heard stirrings in the kitchen, so I went in to greet them and asked, "What would you like for breakfast?"

Timidly Lauren asked, "Would you make us animal pancakes?"

After many years, I knew my efforts were appreciated when from out of nowhere, Richard said, "Mary, my children love you. I think you've made it into the tent!"

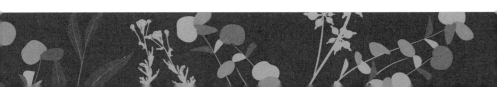

SHARED MOTHERHOOD

Chieko Okazaki

You know the myths—that mothers are always patient and serene, that they always know exactly the right thing to say when those teaching moments come, that they can create homes that are such peaceful refuges from the world that their children will grow up always in tune with the Spirit. These concepts are beautiful ideals that we should cherish and strive for, but they are not accurate pictures of the realities we live in. The belief that we are the only ones in our wards who aren't living the ideals already is what makes these myths dangerous.

There is a beautiful jewel of truth in each of these myths, because motherhood embodies many ideals. Motherhood brings moments of such absolute rightness with the universe that nothing can rival them for sweetness. Motherhood stretches our capacity for love until we begin to comprehend the mysteries of divine love. It reteaches us truths so profound that we could have learned them originally only on the other side of the veil. And it connects us in a web of relationships that instinctively comes to mind when we try to imagine what the joy of heaven will be like.

But there is a way in which these ideals do not serve us well. Sometimes, instead of recognizing them as ideals toward which we should continually strive, we think of them as descriptors of a reality that everybody but us is living. Sometimes as we try to live up to the myth, we just end up feeling guilty. So my vote is for the shared realities of motherhood: real women dealing with real children in a web of shared realities and responsibilities.

Motherhood for me began with a shared rescue that reinforced the concept of accepting many partners in parenting. It was the summer of 1952, and my husband, Ed, and I had been married for three years but had no children. We were living in Salt Lake City, where we had come the previous fall. Ed was working on his master of social work degree at the University of Utah, and I was an exchange teacher at Uintah Elementary School, teaching second grade. When school ended, I looked for a summer job and found the perfect thing for an island girl—lifeguard at the swimming pool in Liberty Park.

In mid-July I was watching the pool when someone came running up, calling that a little boy had drowned. I went immediately to the dressing room, and there was five-year-old Ricky Smith, who was limp and definitely not breathing. I began giving him artificial respiration, and after a few minutes he started breathing again. The ambulance arrived and gave him a few minutes on an inhalator to get his oxygen levels back to normal, and then the crisis was over.

It must have been a slow news day, because Ricky and I had our pictures in the paper. Both of us were in our swimming suits, Ricky slurping down a malted milk while I held him on my lap with my arms around him. I didn't want to let him go. He was so precious to me. Ricky's mother wasn't in the photograph, but she was hovering just barely out of sight, and I imagine there were a few more hugs than usual that afternoon in the Smith household.

Then, in mid-January 1994 when I was speaking to the wives of the Brigham Young University faculty, a woman came up after the program and introduced herself to me. It was Donna Smith! She'd brought a copy of the newspaper clipping—which I didn't have—and a photograph of Rick. To say I was thrilled is putting it mildly. I felt like the shepherd who had been looking for one lamb for almost forty-two years!

I pored over the photograph. Five-year-old Ricky had turned into a tall man, smiling shyly at the camera with his arm around his smiling wife, Lydia, as they stood in front of their home in Lacy, Washington. With them were their three happy children.

"I feel such a heartful of love and gratitude for you every time I see or hear you," Donna Smith wrote me later. "Yes, our lives truly do touch the lives of others."

She gave me Rick's phone number that day, and I called him the next weekend. It was wonderful to hear his voice and complete the circle of caring. When I asked him if he remembered anything about that frightening day in July forty-one years ago, he wasn't sure.

"I think I remember lying on the concrete, but it's kind of hazy," he said. "My mother has told me about it many times, and I'm not sure whether I remember it myself or whether I remember her telling me about it."

He tried in many, many ways to thank me for those few moments of artificial respiration so many years ago. "I have a happy family," he said. "I'm so happy with my wife and my children. I'm so grateful for them. When I think that a five-year-old's life could end—that there might have been nothing in my life after age five—it's kind of scary." He thinks of this, he said, when he looks at his own five-year-old daughter.

He thanked me over and over for calling, but I was thanking him, too. "This completes something for me," I told him. "I've been searching for you! Meeting your mother again and finding you satisfies something that I have wanted to know for forty years. It's like completing a pattern."

I think our lives are connected in ways we don't always understand. One of the things I'm looking forward to about heaven is to see the whole pattern and to see that there are no loose ends from that perspective, to see every relationship as whole and shining, and to truly see how we are all connected with each other.

In terms of motherhood, Donna Smith and I shared her son in a way that made me feel connected to him for almost forty-two years. Now I, a Japanese-American from Hawaii, am happy when I think of a brick home in Lacy, Washington, with a rosebush outside the door, and two parents, happy with their blond and red-headed children. All of us have richer lives because of that sharing.

Even though motherhood, as a mythic image, reduces to one of those beautiful soft-focus photographs of a modern Madonna smiling tenderly over her sleeping baby cradled in her arms, the reality is that motherhood is a web of shared responsibilities. First and foremost, motherhood implies fatherhood as well. I'm glad Rick could tell me he was so happy with Lydia and the children that it scared him a little whenever he thought of that moment in Liberty Park. In fact, it took him a few minutes to come to the phone because he was putting the children to bed.

We share our parenting responsibilities with teachers, with Scoutmasters and Brownie leaders, with music teachers and judo instructors, with ski coaches and librarians, with pediatricians and school counselors, with our children's friends and their parents, and sometimes with other members of their friends' families.

I don't know where women get the idea that mothering is something they have to do all alone. I hope that being able to reconceptualize it as a shared activity will help them feel more realistic about what they can do as mothers for their own children and also more confident about reaching out to mother the children of other women, perhaps in ways that those women can't provide themselves.

I really can't recall hearing very much from

stepmothers or about the process of stepparenting. I think of the enormous burdens and responsibilities on the parents of blended families, how hard the tasks of stepparenting must be, how little help stepparents get, and how little credit they get for their efforts. Thousands of women are helping to raise the children of other women. They are truly unsung heroes, and I wish I knew more about those dynamics.

Motherhood is a complex and powerful experience that elicits a spectrum of human emotions from supreme elation to the depths of despair, from intensely powerful love to equally intense rage. But if one were to tally the sum of these emotions, where would the balance tip?

Remember that you have powerful secret forces working on your side. I refer to the scriptures and to the Atonement of Christ. The scriptures are a treasure-house of information for mothers. They are full of the stories of mothers who weren't perfect—like Sarah and Rebekah—but who loved their children. They tell of mothers like Eve whose faith, even when children went astray, stayed strong in the Lord. The scriptures teach the principles of love, patience, prayer, and courage that family living tests again and again. And perhaps most important, the scriptures testify of Christ and explain the plan of salvation, which are such sturdy anchors to help mothers (and fathers) endure the trials of life and be sources of light and inspiration for their children.

One of the most important things we know about God is that He's a father. That means He has an automatic and intense interest in each child on earth and how that child is parented. I think miracles are available to us. None of us had perfect parents. None of us can be perfect parents while on this earth. But there is a perfect partner in parenting available to us all.

The Savior we love has told us that our Heavenly Father considers the lilies of the field and counts each sparrow. In this system of divine bookkeeping, there is no child who is lost or overlooked, no child who is too insignificant to merit the Father's full love and concern. In this context, it is important to remember that each one of us is also a beloved child, fully in the Father's attention, fully eligible for the Savior's grace, fully capable of achieving godhood with the help of the Savior.

Whether the glorious Second Coming occurs in the span of our mortal lifetime or not, surely we will come before him at the Day of Judgment. We all anticipate that great homecoming at some point in our future when we will again be with the Heavenly Father whom we remember only dimly now except for in those moments of great sweetness and piercing love. And surely that's what we want for our children. As we deal with the realities of our lives, surely that is an ideal worthy of holding before us.

WHAT ARE YOU?

Ardeth G. Kapp

My husband and I do not have any children at the present time. Our blessings in this matter have been delayed. But make no mistake, we are even now a family. Our family unit was established by the authority of God at the same time that we knelt at the altar in the temple. Children come as an extension and expansion of the family. When a man and a woman are married, they immediately become a family and remain a family even in the temporary absence of children.

I mention this because I know many young couples struggle with the sorrow of childlessness. I would like to share with those who have not been blessed with children my testimony and some of my insights gained from personal experience about our particular challenge. Because these experiences are so personal, I have seldom shared them outside the walls of our own home.

Heber and I understand and remember some of the pains and much of the suffering that we endured. We remember the emotional highs and lows with every month, including the fast and testimony meetings when testimonies were borne by those who asked in faith and were blessed with children. We know how it is to return home and put two dinner plates on the table and to recall the marriage covenant to multiply and replenish the earth, and to desire desperately to qualify for that honor in righteousness. We know how it is to not be able to explain our feelings to each other, much less to family and friends; and how one's whole soul cries out as did Job, "If I be righteous, . . . I am full of confusion; therefore see thou mine affliction." (Job 10:15.)

Some go through the suffering and concerns of childlessness year after year until finally they may even say, "My soul is weary of . . . life" (Job 10:1), thinking that if they have no children, they cannot fill the measure of their creation. And if they don't fill the measure of their creation, they may say to themselves, what else matters?

I will forever remember the day a child new to our neighborhood knocked on our door and asked if our children could come out to play. I explained to him, as to others young and old, for the thousandth time, that we didn't have any children. This little boy squinted his eyes in a quizzical look and asked the question I had not dared put into words, "If you are not a mother, then what are you?"

Others have undoubtedly had similar experiences. Mother's Day may be one of those times of hurt. Every year there will be a Mother's Day, and every year at church a little plant or some other gift may be forced into the clenched fist of the woman who has not had a child. But one day she will learn to open her heart, and then, somehow, she will open her hand to receive that gift. Eventually, that gift becomes the symbol of an eternal promise. In these ways we grow from the time when everything hurts and offends us until, with faith in God, we are neither hurt nor offended.

How do we handle unfulfilled expectations? First, we must accept the reality that this life is not intended to be free of struggle. In fact, it is through struggle that we are given opportunities to fulfill the very purpose of this mortal life. It is the fiery trials of mortality that will either consume us or refine us.

Part of those trials is facing alternatives and making decisions. For those of us without children, the choices may seem incredibly difficult to make. What would the Lord have us do? To what extent do we seek medical attention? What about adoption and foster children? What about no children—and if that is the choice, then what do we do with our lives? The choices are never simple. During these times of searching, we often find ourselves caught between conflicting counsel from parents and friends and leaders and doctors and other experts. Some couples I have known even consider divorce, each one thinking the other is responsible.

From my own experience, I've learned that the only lasting peace is the peace that comes when we learn the Lord's will concerning our opportunities in life. To do that, we must consider our alternatives, formulate a decision, and take it to the Lord. We just don't know the Lord's timeline, and that is where our faith comes in.

There will be times when we may feel that our desires are righteous, but the answer is still no. At that point, the only way to peace is to say, "Not my will but thine be done." The Lord doesn't have to explain His decisions to us. If He did, how would we learn faith? I have learned that we must make our choices— even the hard ones—and then accept responsibility for the consequences. It is in facing the awesome responsibility of using our agency and, in faith, making decisions of great eternal consequence, that we are drawn close to God.

Someday, maybe years after the trial of our faith, we will receive a witness that our decisions were right. (See Ether 12:6.) But until then, those who try to live in tune with the promptings of the Spirit must exercise no small degree of faith and courage in following that Spirit.

What, then, are some of the decisions couples can make to lead fulfilled lives when the answer is that they will not have children in this life?

My husband and I knew that parents are constantly placed in situations that help them develop unselfishness and sacrifice. We began to realize that if we were to learn the important lessons that our friends with children were learning, we needed to place ourselves in situations where we could serve and sacrifice. So we began to say yes to everything and to everyone.

It wasn't long before we had many opportunities to serve and sacrifice. Often, at the end of a long week we would plan for a moment together—just the two of us—and the telephone would ring. We'd postpone our moment together and carry on with joyful, grateful hearts for our opportunities.

We who do not have children can wallow in self-pity—or we can experience "birth pains" as we struggle to open the passageway to eternal life for ourselves and others. I bear testimony that instead of wrapping our empty and aching arms around ourselves, we can reach out to others. As we do so, one day we can even be able to hold our friends' babies and rejoice. We can rejoice with the mother of a new bride, and the mother of a newly called missionary, and even with our friends the day they become grandmothers.

I don't know how long it will be for others who have similar longings. For us it was years. But one day we did gain an eternal perspective, and we felt peace, not pain; hope, not despair. I would have liked so much to have received that insight years before, but I know that had that happened, I would have been deprived of the growth that comes from being comforted by the witness of the Spirit after the trial of my faith.

If I have any comforting message for others,

it is this: Peace of mind comes from keeping an eternal perspective. Motherhood, I believe, is a foreordained mission. For some, this glorious blessing may be delayed, but it will not be denied. Motherhood is an eternal reality for all women who live righteously and accept the teachings of the gospel.

On the other hand, the characteristics of motherhood, which include concern for others, sacrifice, service, compassion, teaching, encouraging, and inspiring, can be the noble labor for each of us now, with or without children. The fate of each spirit in the eternities to come depends so much on the training it receives from those here and now who are willing to help another gain eternal life.

To participate in this glorious work gives meaning and purpose, great joy, and eternal blessings each and every day, even as we anticipate the promises of the future.

I have come to know that we can all,
both men and women, rejoice in the
sacred calling of *motherhood*. To give birth
is but one part of this sacred calling.

—ARDETH G. KAPP

I DIDN'T WANT TO LIKE HER

KaRyn Lay

About three years ago, I asked for a priesthood blessing of comfort during a difficult time. Though I was fully expecting the Lord to speak words of affirmation (which He did), I was not expecting what came next. I was distinctly told by the Spirit that the comfort I sought could be found in building a relationship with someone I desperately did *not* want to know—my stepchildren's biological mother.

This?!? This was the road to comfort and peace? I mean, my husband's ex-wife Nikki was great . . . at a comfortable distance where I could sort of pretend she didn't exist.

Let me explain. Some other people in my position might tell you that they never imagined they would end up as a stepparent and that it was never part of their plan. But not me. I truly believe that I was divinely prepared to take on this type of mothering. At a young age, I became obsessed with the idea of adoption and always seemed to visualize my future with ten babies who looked nothing like me or my husband, Brad Pitt. I was single well into my thirties and often dated men who had children from previous relationships. I found it easy to fall in love with children I hadn't borne myself and never felt squeamish at the idea of an insta-family. My longtime obsession with adoption seemed especially merciful when I had a few health issues later in life that curtailed the possibility of bearing children of my own. As compensation, I feel like Heavenly Father made it easy for me to imagine my life as a stepmom. When I met and fell in love with my husband, a huge part of our romance and future revolved around his amazing kids, who were six and eight when we got married. Loving our little insta-family fiercely was the easy part.

What didn't come easily was sharing. Because I will never have biological children of my own, I pour every ounce of my mothering energy into my two stepchildren. There were strange moments when I found myself resentful of the fact that they were not fully "mine." I had all kinds of plans for how I would raise my kids from infancy—what I would teach them, how they would view the world, what I would tell them about life. But they had a mom who was already building that sort of familial infrastructure with them. Intellectually, I understood that I hold a special and unique purpose and place in their lives, but I couldn't help mourning the loss of control that coparenting with another family brings. And though I never expected the kids to ever call me "Mom," it still stung to hear them correct someone who accidentally referred to me as their mother when we were testing out bunk beds at Ikea.

And Nikki was the real mom. The other woman who got first dibs on the macaroni necklaces and handprint Mother's Day art. She was always generous and patient with me as I learned my role, but it was easier on my heart to compartmentalize the two families. Though we never spoke ill of one another and worked hard to never make the kids "take sides," we definitely didn't sit and chat. And now I was being asked to develop a friendship. Why? Why would the Lord ask me to step up in this way when He knew it would require serious heart-stretching?

Well, I may be stubborn, but when the Spirit reveals something to me that strongly, I can't ignore it. So the next time I texted Nikki about drop-offs and pickups, I asked her if she had some time to talk with me . . . about the kids. I just couldn't bring myself to say, "I want us to be friends." That felt too needy. Too weird or lacking in boundaries. I often tried to put myself in her shoes and I could only imagine the mental and emotional gymnastics it takes to let your children love another "mother" even if it has the word "step" in front of it. I recalled all the times I had done things that must have felt frustrating to her and the few times when I *knew* I had stepped on her toes. That almost derailed me in my effort to develop a friendship. I'm deeply afraid of not being liked!

But as I prayed fervently during the drive to her

house, my mind also recalled the times when she had been generous and forgiving of my failures. I was reminded that we both are women of God who believe in Him and His divine plan of happiness. We both have made and work toward keeping covenants with our Father in Heaven to "mourn with those that mourn; yea, and comfort those that stand in need of comfort" (Mosiah 18:9), and that includes one another. That covenant does not exclude any group or person, no matter how uncomfortable it may be. Most importantly, we both love these children who didn't ask for any of this.

Our children. God's children.

I took courage and kept on driving.

Our first conversation may have felt tentative, cautious, guarded (at least from my perspective!), but they didn't stay that way. Though we are careful to avoid subjects that don't engender loyalty to our spouses, Nikki has truly become, as the Lord promised, a comfort to me. She is able to laugh with us about the crazy things the kids do and we can share the things we're learning about parenting when we sit next to each other for two hours of our lives that we can never get back at the elementary school talent show. Because I know her better, I now understand how her presence in my life is giving me freedom to be the mother I always hoped to be instead of blocking it.

I knew that something amazing was happening when my stepdaughter cheerfully declared to someone that her mom and I were friends and asked if I was going to come in and hang out during a routine drop-off. Together, Nikki and I are working to shape the lives of two human beings who need what each of us has to offer. And in the process, we are honoring our commitment to true discipleship. I believe we are living unto the Lord in this small but important way.

I understand that a relationship like this is not possible or even advisable for everyone in a similar situation, and my heart aches for my sisters who are struggling to find peace in their step-parenting role. To be honest, I don't know if I would have sought it out without such a strong prompting from God. But I do know that each of us will absolutely be asked to step out of our comfort zone as we seek to arise and live unto the Lord. It's just part of the process. And in presenting us with what I like to call our "Divine Friction," He will also *absolutely* guide us to the source of all comfort and courage, our Redeemer Jesus Christ. It is our challenge and privilege to accept His guidance and choose to grow.

AN INDIVIDUAL PURPOSE

Patricia T. Holland

In a poignant exchange with God, Adam stated that he would call the woman "Eve." And why did he call her Eve? "Because she was the mother of all living" (Genesis 3:20; Moses 4:26).

As I tenderly acknowledge the very real pain that many single women, or married women who have not borne children, feel about any discussion of motherhood, could we consider this one possibility about our eternal female identity—our unity in our diversity. Eve was given the identity of the mother of all living—years, decades, perhaps centuries before she had ever borne a child. It would appear that her motherhood preceded her maternity just as surely as the perfection of the Garden preceded the struggles of mortality. I believe *mother* is one of those very carefully chosen words, one of those words rich with meaning after meaning after meaning. We must not, at all costs, let that word divide us. I believe with all my heart that it is first and foremost a statement about our nature, not a head count of our children. I have only three children and have wept that I could not have eight. (Some of you may have eight and weep that you can't have three.) And I know that some of you without any have wept too. And sometimes, too many have simply been angry over the very subject itself. For the sake of our eternal motherhood I plead that this not be so.

Some women give birth and raise children but never "mother" them. Others, whom I love with all my heart, "mother" all their lives but have never given birth. Therefore, we must understand that however we accomplish it, parenthood is the highest of callings, the holiest of assignments. And all of us are Eve's daughters, married or single, maternal or barren, every one of us. We are created in the image of the Gods to become gods and goddesses. And we can provide something of that divine pattern, that maternal prototype, for each other and for those who come after us. Whatever our circumstance, we can reach out, touch, hold, lift, and nurture—but we cannot do it in isolation. We need a community of sisters stilling the soul and binding the wounds of fragmentation.

I know that God loves us individually and collectively—as women—and that He has a personal mission, an individual purpose for every one of us. As I learned on my Galilean hillside, I testify that if our desires are righteous, God overrules for our good and will tenderly attend to our needs. In our diversity and individuality, my prayer is that we will be united— united in seeking our specific, foreordained mission, united in asking not "What can the kingdom do for me?" but "What can I do for the kingdom? How do I fulfill the measure of *my* creation? In my circumstances and my challenges and with my faith, where is my *full* realization of the godly image in which I was created?"

With faith in God, His prophets, His Church, and ourselves—faith in our own divine creation—may we be peaceful and let go of our cares and troubles over so many things. May we believe—nothing doubting—in the light that shines, even in a dark place.

We are the Lord's disciples. He accepts us as we are, even as we are growing toward what we must become. Rest in that love. Bathe and luxuriate in it. Let it relax, calm, and comfort you. Let us keep our face to the Son and come unto Him.

FIVE LESSONS OF LOVE

Elaine Cannon

I once had to shut myself and our four little ones under six into the nursery. I had a fever of 104 degrees, and I was pregnant again. Staying upright was no longer a viable option. In my misery I curled up on a youth bed to keep a watchful eye on our precious destroying angels. Balls and baby bottles sailed over my head while dark thoughts stirred my mind. My young husband was a conscientious new bishop who was always visiting the sick, and I wondered how sick one had to be to get the bishop to come and call in our home!

I didn't feel like much of a mother—more like a big baby, such was my self-pity.

Then the doorbell rang, and I dragged from the bed to peer through the window to the front porch. There stood the Relief Society president, an older woman who worked closely with my young husband in the welfare needs of our ward. She was old enough to be my mother, and I was appalled that she should catch me in my failure, in this house of chaos where no mother's hand had been raised recently to do more than keep the little ones from hurting each other.

The stampede to answer the doorbell came from children aching for release from the confinement of the nursery. While I called through the window that I was ill and would see her another time, the children were already opening the door for her.

Then the most marvelous bit of "other mothering" occurred. This time I was the child being taught lifesaving lessons. This fine friend explained that she had been driving by our house and had felt prompted by the Spirit that help was needed therein.

Lesson one: Be in tune and respond to the promptings of the Spirit.

She had hurried home to get her ever-ready Friendship Bag, full of supplies and surprises for the sick and afflicted.

Lesson two: Be prepared and equipped to meet the need.

Returning to our home, she rang the doorbell until there was a response.

Lesson three: Don't give up too soon in doing your good deeds!

She told me to lie down on the living room couch while she lured the children to the kitchen table with cookies and new coloring books. She would help me in a moment. In relief, I obeyed.

Lesson four: Even a mother needs a mother on occasion.

Sister Jensen took my foot in her hands, ignoring my protests of embarrassment that she would be doing that to *me*! She talked quietly and comfortingly, all the while massaging each foot while she healed my soul. There was quiet for a moment, and then I got lesson five: "Love your partner, Elaine. Love him enough so that he has plenty to give his ward members. Let your bishop-husband be a good shepherd."

When It's Hard

PEACE IN THE LEARNING

Emily Belle Freeman

He is three years old. The two of us walk out of the hospital, out of the place of celebration. Today it is the place where new life, a newborn son, my nephew, has entered the world to find peace nestled in his mother's arms. As we walk outside, Josh complains about how the light hurts his eyes, it hurts his head. He whimpers and reaches his arms up, "Hold to you, Mommy," he says the way he always does, and I lift him into my arms the way I always do.

Josh and I get to the car and what was a whimper has turned into full tears, and as I buckle him in he begs me to cover his head with a cream and crimson blanket, the fringe around the edges sitting softly there on his lap. I tell myself he is tired; I tell myself he is cranky from waiting in the lobby for too many hours with his dad while I celebrated the beginning of new life upstairs. But as we pull onto the freeway he begins to throw up. I try to talk to him, try to help him, but he doesn't respond. I am in the middle of the freeway, and I don't know what to do, and through the closed eyes and the throwing up he just whimpers; he won't stop whimpering. Until there is silence, and I drive to the only place I can think of for an emergency like this, and for some reason it isn't the hospital I just left. I drive to the office of my pediatrician, and I stand on the sidewalk, and I hold him unconscious in my arms, and I pound hard on the glass door because it is lunchtime and they have locked the door.

The details aren't important now. How they finally let us in and put us in a room. How I stripped him down to his navy blue and green plaid boxers and put all of his soaked-through belongings into a trash bag. How the soft pink sweater I was wearing reeked of the reality of whatever was going on. *What was going on?* How, in that wild moment, his doctor walked in from lunch and saw us sitting in the tiny room on the blue chair. Josh, fully unclothed and curled up into the pain and me trying to hold all of the pain and the unanswered questions and the fear—oh, the fear. How the doctor took one look at us and said, "It is diabetes. He has diabetes." And how a room was reserved for us at the children's hospital where we would go for five days and learn how to manage a disease we didn't want to have.

Five days later we leave the hospital and Josh thinks he is better. We walk out into the bitter November air and he clutches his teddy bear with his right fist and my hand with his left. He is happy, and I buckle him in his seat, and I sigh—we are going home. It is lunchtime when we get there. I unbuckle him from the seat and begin to unload everything from the car. He is not happy when he sees it—the needles, the meters, and the lancets that have become our reality, our way of life. He doesn't want that life. They let us go home from the hospital, and he is better now, and he doesn't need those things.

Josh is starving, and I lift him up on the counter to prick his little finger so it will bleed and tell him how the food he wants to eat will affect his tiny body. He starts crying the moment I pull out the black kit we brought home from the hospital. He squeezes his little hand into a fist and cries hot, angry tears. "I hate this." His mad voice is new; it came home with us from the hospital with all of the baggage we didn't want. "I hate you," he says, hot tears streaming down red cheeks. "You don't do this to anyone else in our family. You only do this to me. Why did you ever think I wanted to do this?"

I hold his hand tight, pulling his little fingers open, and send a sharp prick into his baby skin. Red blood pools, and I drip it onto the meter and hold him there while I ready the shot. He grabs my cheeks with both hands as the needle enters his thigh, and he pinches me just as hard as he can. I feel his fingernails in my cheeks, I feel them breaking through the skin underneath the hot tears running down, I feel the sting of the salt, and still, I let him pinch me. I am hurting him. He has every right to hurt me back. When the shot is empty, I set him down on the floor so I can get his lunch, and he runs up the stairs, runs down the hallway, runs into his room and slams the door.

I sit down in the middle of the tile on my kitchen floor and weep.

You can't explain health to a three-year-old. You can't explain that you making him bleed three times a day, four times a day, eight times a day is keeping him alive. There is no logic in the tiny mind of a young boy who doesn't understand why his mother wants to hurt him, keeps hurting him, a mother who will continue to hurt him every day for the rest of his life. I sob. There is nothing else to do but cry.

That night I tuck the boys into their beds. I pull the blue and green comforters up and they are cozy and warm, and I long for their quiet, peaceful sleep. I snuggle my daughter Megan as I rock her in the rocking chair. Her calm breathing calms my troubled heart, and when she has settled completely, I gently lay her in the waiting crib. I say good night to Greg, hear him roll over, hear the steady breathing begin. I have learned that these times, these are the best times to cry. The times when nobody knows. So they don't have to be frightened, so they don't carry the weight, so that in the daylight they might think things are getting better.

I lie motionless in my bed and stare at the ceiling as the tears run from the corners of my eyes and into the flannel pillowcase. I try to think through all the people in my life—surely there must be someone who would know how to help me get out of this place, this dark place, this place where I don't want to be. For an hour I cry and I think through the names of every single person I know. Surely there is someone. But at the end I take a deep, sob-racked breath and I realize what I have known all along. I am alone in this. I am alone.

I have been in this alone place before, so this time it isn't long before the realization settles in. I am not alone in this. *He knows.* God knows. I am certain of this. So I begin to pray, and even though He already knows everything, I start at the very beginning and I tell Him all of it. How much it hurts, how heavy the burden is that I carry daily, how exhausted I am from the weight of it. As I pour out my heart, I pray for the relief that is promised in Matthew 11: "Come unto me, all ye that labour and are heavy laden, and I will give you rest. Take my yoke upon you, and learn of me; for I am meek and lowly in heart: and ye shall find rest unto your souls" (Matthew 11:28–29). The tears continue to fall, and I plead with Him for this rest.

I feel peace. It enters the room quiet, but thick, the comfort of it settling soft. I stop praying; I rest in the peace. All night long I rest in the peace. The next morning I pick up the burden and prepare to begin again, but this time I notice it is lighter. With time I learn that what will get me through the day, each dark day, is knowing the night will come, and with it the opportunity to pour out my heart in prayer again. To rest in Him. Those nighttime conversations become the balm that carries me through.

Years go by, and Josh is twelve. His diabetes has become a way of life. We are used to it—as used to it as we can be. Josh and I have been asked to participate in a research study at the University of Utah. They are following adolescents who have diabetes. It is a four-year study. They want to see how having this disease will affect Josh, how it will affect us. Being there makes me remember our reality.

I am in one room with a social worker, and Josh is in another. We each have a test in front of us, filled with multiple-choice questions. The test will take at least an hour to complete. I begin the questions, and they are easy, and I think that I will finish faster than they expect. But then I get to one question I can't answer, and I pause. I sit there for a long time before the social worker finally asks if I need help.

"I don't know if I can answer this question," I tell her. I have been struggling with it for ten minutes, and I can't decide how to respond.

"It's all right," she assures me. "Just initial it so we know you read it and you can leave it blank."

But I can't. I have to figure out the answer. The unknowing doesn't sit well with me.

The question says, "If you knew it meant you would

have to give up all of the learning, would you choose to never have had your child diagnosed with diabetes?"

Of course the right answer is yes. It's so easy. I shouldn't even have to think about it. But *all of the learning*—that is the part that holds me back.

I think about the conversations Josh and I have had. Because of this, he has learned to have empathy for those who are different, his heart goes out to the one; he is known for this. I think of how he holds on to the verse in Joshua, "Be strong and of a good courage" (Joshua 1:8) He thinks it was written for him; he has thought that since he was three. I think of how he has learned to lean on Jesus, to find strength in Him.

As I look back I realize that this learning hasn't only been good for Josh.

I remember those late nights in my bedroom, the conversations that I looked forward to during those dark days, the moments when I poured out my heart in prayer to Him. I remember the peace, the way the burden seemed to be lighter every morning, and I realize I can't give those memories up. Those late nights, those intimate moments when I had learned to trust God, were too precious to me. And I realize the truth I never thought I would arrive at.

I am not willing to give up the learning.

It dawns on me that sometimes the places of deepest hurt allow us to forge the bonds of deepest trust.

I am reminded of the scripture in Psalms, "Deep calleth unto deep" (Psalm 42:7). It's true. You only trust Him as deeply as you need Him. And I needed Him in this. Desperately needed Him. I called to Him from the depths of despair, and He gave me reason to trust.

As we look around at other mothers,
it is easy to see the best and finest in them. Then
we *compare* that seemingly perfect person with
ourselves at our worst. It often appears that no one
else has problems. But everyone does. Don't shackle
your forward progress by negative thoughts.

MARILYNNE TODD LINFORD

HAPPINESS ON THE HARD ROAD

Linda S. Reeves

Many years ago now, when I had just four young children—in fact, our oldest was not quite five (I had always looked forward to motherhood and loved those little children)—I was overwhelmed. My house was almost always a mess, and often the children were not dressed until noon. If they had been fed at all, it was because they'd gone on into the kitchen and gotten themselves cold cereal. But I realized I was not enjoying motherhood, mainly because I didn't like the mother that I was. I was having a hard time maintaining control, being happy, and accomplishing all that I felt like I needed to do. I found myself with a desperate feeling. I wasn't alone in this—my husband was feeling the same way. We were both overwhelmed. So we determined that we would spend some time over the next little while in fervent prayer to our Heavenly Father and that our scripture study would be with the end in mind of finding out what the Lord would have us do so that we could get things under control. We went to the temple and we pled with the Lord over a period of months. And the answer that came was really so simple, and something that we hear all the time. In fact, I've been so touched by those that have spoken today, seeing that the revelation that comes from our Heavenly Father, what our prophets, seers, and revelators have told us, is truly the same for all of us. What came to me and to my husband was that every day we needed to have our personal prayers and prayer with our children. Every day, we needed to read the scriptures individually and also with our children. Each Monday night—you know the answer to that one—family home evening. We should also try to get to the temple as often as we could, even with those four little children.

Now does this mean that nothing else was important? Certainly there are other important things—service is very important. But the Lord was telling us to prioritize, to concentrate on those four things. Do those all-important things every day, and everything else that's important will fall into place. I've even had women who knew me well, who said years later, "Oh, Linda, I remember coming to your home and ringing the doorbell and one of the children would come in the door, and if they had any clothes on at all it was just underwear." When they've told me that, the thought would come into my mind, *Yes, but did you know that we had prayer and read scriptures that day?* And you know, when I say that things haven't been easy, believe me, they haven't. It's been a hard road, and we've had some good adversity. But the confidence before the Lord, and the sweetness that has come into our lives as I've seen our children come to know the Savior, to really know who He is, and to know of His Atonement, because we tried to read the scriptures, and we were praying, as I look over and watch them and see that they're trying to do the same things that we did, there is so much peace and happiness in my life.

BUILDING A NEW LIFE

Kimberley Burton Heuston

One of the most precious legacies of our Heavenly Parents is the power we each carry to create and re-create our life stories. The flip side of the dislocation of bereavement or divorce is the tremendous freedom and flexibility of vision that can come with the construction of a new life. As we shift through the shards of the old life now splintered beyond repair, we ask ourselves over and over, "What is the best part? What is worth saving? What concerns and projects should be put aside for another day?"

At the same time, we are aware as never before of our personal weaknesses. We chose our partners not only because they were pleasing to us but also because they were the mothers or the fathers we wanted for our children. Without their strengths to fortify us and to shore up our weaknesses, it seems as though we will do nothing but founder about helplessly, mired in the muck of our foolish inadequacies.

This feeling of being stuck is a familiar one to those who have struggled to overcome a bad habit or repent of a tenacious sin.

And the promise that delivers us is the same: "If it so be that the children of men keep the commandments of God he doth nourish them, and strengthen them, and provide means whereby they can accomplish the thing which he has commanded them" (1 Nephi 17:3). That is the Lord's promise to us; it is the very fabric of His work and his glory, which is "to bring to pass the immortality and eternal life of man" (Moses 1:39).

If we are hungering for a more excellent way, for a life that is more full of light and goodness than our own, we have been given the instruction we need to obtain it. First, we must do all that we can. Then we must ask the Lord in faith for help and wait on His good time.

Six or seven years ago, at the most difficult moment of my own divorce, I sat in a sacrament meeting and heard a man in his mid-thirties bear his testimony. "Four years ago," he said, "I had hit bottom. My marriage had ended, and my ex-wife had custody of our daughter. I did not know that it was possible to feel that much pain and still survive. Today, I am married to a wonderful new wife who loves my daughter, and today we blessed her little sister who will keep us company when she goes home to her mom. I didn't know that it was possible to be this happy on this side of the veil."

Hearing that testimony was a bittersweet experience for me. On the one hand, it seemed yet another expression of the gulf that seemed to lie between me and all those happy people out there. At the same time, it offered an implied promise that happiness would eventually come to me, as indeed it has.

It has not come in the way I expected, which is to say in the wake of a worthy partner who loves and cherishes me and my children. Although I hope and believe that I will be married again in the Lord's due time, I am beginning to settle expansively and a bit creakily into middle age, and it is clear that there are experiences that my children and I will never have. They will never know the daily blessing of a father whose life revolves around loving and serving them, their mother, and his God. Likewise, I will never be the full-time mother I had hoped and planned to be. My future husband will never see or know me as the trim and radiant young woman I once was, and will never know the fat cheeks and great listening eyes of my children's babyhoods. There are parts of my life as a woman and a mother that no one on earth will ever share.

Some of these parts are worth knowing, worth sharing. When I see something that is beautiful to me, I have a habit of stretching my hand out to the side, hoping there will be someone to take it. Sometimes I feel a child seize it, and that is a delight. More often, it stays empty. Six or seven years ago, its emptiness was reason for tears. Today, instead of reminding me of my solitude, my hand swinging free triggers the accumulated memories of all the other times I have glimpsed and cherished beauties that manifested the Lord's presence. It reminds me that I am not walking alone and that, despite my fears, I never have and never will. I feel a familiar sense of abundance and well-being nestling a little more comfortably around my heart and soul, and I know it is because I am slowly learning what is—and isn't—required to make myself whole according to the gentle instructions of a perfectly wise and loving Friend.

LETTER FROM
A BIRTH MOTHER

Anonymous

Dear Kim:

The most wonderful thing happened to me today. I received a very special phone call. It was from your mother. What a surprise and what a wonderful person she is. She told me many interesting things about you—how pretty you are and sweet and kind; how your brothers and sisters look up to you. Thank you for being that kind of girl.

I truly hope that I may say some things in this letter that will be of comfort to you. I was given the unique experience of bringing you into this life. I never did see you, but I knew you were a choice spirit all the time I was carrying you within me.

At the time I became pregnant with you, I was not married. I fell deeply in love with a man and became pregnant. I wanted to get married *very much*, but he decided to marry somebody else.

At this time, I had been divorced from my first husband for three years. I had two little girls who had missed having their daddy because he never came to see them. Sometimes people are very selfish and they can only think of themselves. That is how their father was, and I saw the pain it caused. I wanted a better life for you. I wanted you to have both a loving mom and dad. I wanted your parents to be married in the temple. I wanted you to be sealed to them. That's how much I loved *you!*

Some people seem to think a mother doesn't love her child when she decides to have the child adopted. But I feel that most mothers who really care and who really love the child have the child adopted because they *love* that child more than themselves!

I loved you, all through my pregnancy, and I loved you when you were born. I love you still today. I didn't see you at birth because I knew that if I did, I wouldn't be able to let you go. My parents—your grandparents—did get to see you. Your grand-mother wanted to make sure you were all right. And she told me you were. She told me you were a beautiful girl, just as your mother told me today. Your parents must love you a great deal to allow themselves to contact me.

At first, the heartache of not being able to see you and hold you in my arms and to rear you was unbearable. As the years have gone on, I have tried to think of your happiness with your family now, and I have prayed for strength, and I know Heavenly Father has given me comfort for doing the right thing for you.

Remember the story in the Bible of the two women who fought over their child? And King Solomon told the women that if they were going to fight he would

113

cut the baby in half, and give each a half! Then the real mother stood up and told the king to give the baby to the other woman rather than destroy it. King Solomon knew who the real mother was then.

Another story from the Bible tells of a Hebrew woman who put her baby in a basket among the reeds by a riverbank to save him from being killed along with other infants. And that baby was raised in a royal family and grew up to become Moses!

Even in biblical times, there were mothers who felt it was better for someone else to raise and care for their children. But the mother never stopped loving them or missing them. In the two stories I've mentioned, both of these mothers wanted their children spared from pain and sorrow. They wanted a better life for their child than they could have with them at this time. They wanted this enough to give them away.

Someday, when Heavenly Father wants and the time is right, we will meet in person. Thank you for your life and for caring about me.

WHEN GOD PUTS YOU IN THE STANDBY LINE

Breaunna Stone

In September 2015, we found out I was pregnant. It was one of the happiest moments of my life. I have always wanted to be a mom and feel that motherhood is why God put me on this earth. At my ten-week appointment, our little one was found lifeless inside. Needless to say, we were devastated.

The next May, another ten-week appointment rolled around. This time a strong 180 beats per minute flashed on the monitor. We could not contain our excitement and enthusiasm for a healthy baby. Less than a week later, labor began and we again went through the painful process of losing yet another baby.

When I miscarried my babies, I was in complete despair. I lost my purpose and my confidence and felt stripped of everything that made me who I am.

I began to wonder why we'd had such strong spiritual convictions to start our family early in life, only to have all those hopes crushed.

On many occasions, I felt like God had put me in the standby line. I felt like I was constantly standing by for the blessings of full-term pregnancy and of motherhood. Maybe I was on standby because I needed to learn patience or to feel the kind of pain and grief that cripples you, then builds you into something new.

But waiting is hard. That standby line seems to go on forever. While waiting for God's plan to unfold, I've learned a few things. I firmly believe that one of the biggest reasons for trial and tribulation is to refine and polish you to make you into something better.

While in that standby line, I also learned that I had a choice. I could be miserable and unhappy or I could turn things around and learn something from this experience. I had a marriage to cultivate, and a life to keep living for my Heavenly Father. My choice was to love my babies from this side of the veil and to never forget the blessing they are in my life.

I chose to be happy.

I have come to recognize the blessings of being in the standby line—one of which is the power of God to spiritually heal us. Through devotion to my faith, the powers of heaven have made my broken heart whole again.

As my place in the standby line continued for years, I clung to the knowledge that families are forever. I knew that one day, the blessings of motherhood would come—and they did, just in a way I never expected. Whether it was in this life or in heaven, I knew my time in the standby line would end.

Our own *example* of patience
and trust and endurance when
"the winds blow" will likely be of the
greatest help to our children when
they have their personal trials.

—JOY F. EVANS

ANNIE'S VOICE

Michelle Schmidt

It was a crisp fall morning, and the sky was clear and crystal blue after the storms of the previous day. And though the sky was clear, a mist and a scattering of intermittent clouds dotted the mountains to the right of the gorge. The colors were the most vibrant greens and blues I had ever seen. The river to my left was striking, lined on either side with gorgeous deep green trees. And the mountains to my right were stunning, with waterfalls, moss-covered mountainsides, and huge trees that overwhelmed my ability to take it all in. Even now, I'm completely unable to describe with mere words the beauty of the Columbia River Gorge.

When the reality of what I was seeing overcame me, and I felt a deep spiritual awe at the overwhelming beauty, I spontaneously said, "Oh, Annie! I get it. I'm blown away at how beautiful this place is. No wonder you love it so much. No wonder you wanted me to see this so badly."

And, as unexpectedly as I spoke to her, she spoke back, saying,

"I know, Mom. I told you it was so beautiful! I'm so happy you are able to see this and to love it the way I do."

I held very still, realizing I had experienced a moment that would take me a minute to understand, just like when I was a little girl saying my "thank-you" prayers and heard Heavenly Father speak to me. I thought to myself, "I just heard and felt Annie speak to me. It was every bit my Annie. She was so excited and animated and responded exactly how Annie would have if she had been here in real life."

It *was* Annie's voice, and we'd had a perfect conversation. But there was one problem. If I had truly been able to hear Annie's voice, it was because she was in the spirit world, no longer alive on this earth.

And yet, the voice I'd heard, Annie's voice, hadn't seemed alarmed or distressed in any way. She hadn't seemed worried that she had passed on. Instead, she was ecstatic that I was overcome with the beauty around us, just as much as she was. It was a bonding experience, and I felt a deep connection of love between us. Most important, it filled me with a calm peace and assurance that Annie was completely fine. She wasn't suffering or in pain. She was happy.

As a mother facing days and weeks ahead of searching for my missing daughter, days filled with speculation and all kinds of insinuations surrounding her disappearance by so many well-intentioned people, this one short moment with

Annie's spirit brought me more comfort and strength and peace than I can possibly describe.

That isn't to say that I didn't feel sick in my stomach anytime someone questioned why we had ruled out "foul play" as the cause of Annie's disappearance. And yes, it was hard when someone would call the police saying they had just seen Annie on a bus heading south in California, or some such thing, as if there still might be a glimmer of hope that she was alive.

Yet, for the most part, my experience of hearing Annie's voice and knowing that she was in the spirit world gave me an inner knowledge and peace that my little girl was completely fine, and that what we were searching for was just her physical body.

Until then, I had never realized how precious that physical body was to me. More than anything, I wanted to find that body and bring it safely home. I wanted the closure that it would bring to be able to bury her body, kind of like tucking a child securely into bed at night.

At one point, I remember reasoning with Heavenly Father, telling Him, "I helped create that body. Do I have any claim to it? Because if I do, will you please lead us to it?"

When the first search began and the on-camera interviews ensued, which were so surreal and raw, I was unguarded, vulnerable, unscripted, unable to pretend that I believed Annie was still alive. I was criticized for some of the initial interviews I gave because of it. I understand why that would be upsetting to people. I'm sure I appeared unfeeling as a mother to express a belief that my daughter was dead without showing signs of losing my mind. But the personal witness I had received that we were searching just for Annie's body, and that she was safe and happy in the spirit world, gave me the greatest peace and comfort.

At one point in the day somebody said to me, "I sure hope this has a good outcome." I thought to myself, "It will. The outcome is guaranteed. Christ made sure of that long ago. He has guaranteed our outcome."

PERSPECTIVE ON PAIN

Melissa Wei-Tsing Inouye

I lie here thinking about how you came to me. It took a long time. It started last Sunday night. I was up all night with contractions that came and went every ten minutes or so. Then they disappeared Monday morning. On Monday afternoon I walked for about ten miles or so to try to get them to return. Finally on Monday evening the midwife went ahead and induced labor.

As the contractions began to be more frequent, to exert more force, and to be more painful, I welcomed them. This meant that they were finally doing the work of labor. I lay on my side, breathing slowly, trying to relax, while the contraction began with a slight tightening and quickly ramped up with incredible power. It felt as if my womb were wringing itself out.

When the pain was especially bad I thought about Mom, your grandmother, who was in agonizing, constant pain for the last several months of her life due to a rare cancer of the bile duct.

When I had this thought the contraction would suddenly feel less painful. Then it would subside completely, and I would rest.

There is a point in labor when the entire process becomes completely overwhelming, when the pressure feels unbearable, when you don't know what to do or how you are going to cope for another second. The surges feel like thousands of pounds of pressure smashing down, all at once, with no sign of relief or escape. In these most intense moments one feels despair and begins to believe that perhaps the baby will actually never be born.

I yelled as your head came out. The rest of you soon followed. All of a sudden there was no more pain. It had been so very difficult, so overwhelming, and then it was over. What an absolutely amazing contrast. I was so pleased to hold you in my arms, to see that you stopped crying almost immediately, to smell your hair and put you to my breast. I almost couldn't believe that it was all over, that the hard work of hours and months was done and that I finally had you, my baby, in my arms.

OUR BODIES,
OUR BOOK OF LIFE

Tessa Meyer Santiago

Perhaps one of the most discouraging struggles women endure is that never-ending battle with our own bodies. A woman's attitude toward her own body is fraught with misconceptions fueled by a world that celebrates an almost prepubescent female body as the ideal norm. Unfortunately for most of us, time moves on. We are no longer seventeen, a number of children have made their way through our birth canals, and gravity is exerting its inexorable pull. Whenever we look in the mirror, we are reminded of what we are not. Satan would have it just that way. He would have us think that because our bodies do not look a certain, supposedly desirable, way, they are not worth having at all. Thus, we enter into a war with our bodies, hating the very tabernacle our Father has given us, despising the flesh. If Satan can get us to fixate on our bodies, either in vanity or self-loathing, then he has caused us to misunderstand completely the role our bodies play in our salvation.

I was pregnant all one summer. I spent my time bobbing in

the deep end of Deseret Towers' pool watching the women go by. I wondered why the women who had contributed the most to our society seemed to feel the least confident. Why did they cover their bodies as if in shame, disrobing only to plunge quickly down, their shoulders barely emerging above the waterline as they stood watching their children swim? Why did the freshman Deseret Towers' residents, young women who knew nothing of what breasts and hips and wombs are meant to do, rule, queens of the roost? In a better world, in a kinder, more saintly world, a mother's body would be kindly regarded, with respect and honor for what she has given, for what she has done. I am learning that a woman who mothers well gives all she has: body parts, internal organs, limbs. Some parts are temporarily donated; others, irreparably altered; most effects are permanent. And, if she lets this mothering sink into the marrow of her bones, if she allows the job of nurturing to wrestle with her spirit, a woman's soul is wrought in the image of God.

For me, having a woman's body has meant special tutoring in life and death. I have been pregnant four times. Each pregnancy ended in a surgical procedure. Three times out of four, my stomach and uterus have been cut open to retrieve, in all their bloody splendor, Julia, Christian, and Seth. Each time, I have entered the mother's valley of death, bringing my body under the knife, to lie still as someone cut into my flesh to release life from my womb. What should be a joyous moment is full of fear for me. At the birth of Seth, our youngest, I lay on the operating table trying so very hard to be brave. But I was petrified, and my body knew it: my pulse raced, I hyperventilated and vomited in an allergic reaction to the epidural. My eyes filled with tears. On one level, I desperately wanted to run from that certainty of pain and possibility of death. Yet I had no other choice if I wanted the life within me to live.

As I lay on the table, my mind filled with the image of Annie Dillard's tomcat, who would jump through her bedroom window at night covered with the blood of his kill. When she awoke she would find herself "covered with paw prints in blood." "I looked as though I'd been painted with roses," she recalled. Annie would ask herself, "What blood was this, and what roses? It could have been the rose of union, the blood of murder, or the rose of beauty bare and the blood of some unspeakable sacrifice or birth," (*Pilgrim at Tinker Creek*, 1974). She never knew exactly how to read "the midnight canvas." And I never know when I am on that delivery table exactly what is happening to me. Am I the site of some unspeakable horror or some unspeakable joy? Paradoxically, I am both: An open womb, a uterus pulled out onto my abdomen; an immense pressure, an indignant cry, and a wrinkled old man's face that looks at me from beneath the hospital beanie like a Sharpei puppy. Only after I place my swollen, reluctant body on the table can I hear those first sounds of life. And no, the recovery is never swift in return for my heroism. My stomach has been bisected, the severed nerves need to learn to stop screaming. My bowels remain sluggish from the epidural; my head pounds from the allergic reaction I have known was coming since my first pregnancy.

As I battle through the pains, my body begins to make milk for the child who needs to be fed. When I am barely coherent, unable to sit up, the nurses bring my newborn to me. "He's hungry," they say. "Put him to the breast." So I struggle upright, ignoring the burning incision, to cradle the little body that was so recently inside me. I turn his mouth to me and do for my son what he cannot do for himself. And I understand a little more now how the Savior would "take upon him death, that he may loose the bands of death which bind his people" (Alma 7:12). The demands and duties of life, of the soul, take precedence over the travails of the body.

The third of my four pregnancies ended in death. On a long November Monday morning, I labored for ten hours, knowing that the end would produce only the misshapen fetus that my body in its wisdom knew to expel. While my body tried to perform the labor which it knew was necessary, my spirit keened. Medicine calls it a spontaneous abortion. But I have no name for the desolate feeling that clouded my spirit as my body labored. I knew only my baby would not be born the same week my Emperor tulips were scheduled to appear. I knew I could reshelve the baby name books and stop doodling

"Nicholas Kevin Santiago" on sacrament meeting programs. I knew my sister-in-law and I would not give my parents their twelfth and thirteenth grandchildren a mere three weeks apart after all. But most of all, I knew I wanted with all my heart to have this child, and I grieved for what was not to be.

But I did not grieve alone. In that valley of desolation brought on by physical travail, I believe the Savior sent angels to be with me, to succor me in my infirmity: My sister who rubbed my back, changed the bath water, and who, while I was at the hospital, cleaned my house, did my laundry, and fed my children; nurses who looked at me with compassion, calling me "dear, sweet Tess," their words a consolation, "how sorry I am you are here"; women, who knew and had also labored in vain, whose eyes looked at me with a special sweetness; a doctor who, sensitive to my pain, chose to shield me from a surgical procedure in the sterility of his office and instead administered a blissful ignorance through anesthesia as he cleaned my womb of what had been the promise of a child. Most comforting of all, the Lord gave me a husband who held my hand and stood by, waiting and watching, feeling helpless to stop my pain, wishing he could endure for me. I found him sobbing in his office three days later; he too had lost a child. In all my pain, no one had noticed his. Yet, I believe we both felt the arms of the Savior around us healing our hearts in the aftermath of that dreadful week. We felt our neighbors' tears, their hearts aching, sorrowing for our pain; we heard the faint whisperings of another child in time; we learned lessons in patience from Him who would gather us in his arms as a mother hen would gather her chicks.

Could I have broken my heart to the will of the Lord another way? Would I have come so heavy laden and willingly to the Savior's yoke? I don't know. I do know that the death of a small, misshapen body brought light to my soul that perhaps could not have entered any other way. I cannot help but think, as I remember those births, that this human body, also can make us most divine—that the peculiar pains of a woman's flesh teach her exquisitely, intimately. What they teach she cannot know beforehand or even know that she needs to know. But when the pain subsides or is grown accustomed to, she realizes that some time during the darkest of nights or mundanest of mornings, knowledge has descended like the dews from heaven and enlarged her soul.

Unfortunately, the experience has also enlarged her hips and thighs. If she's anything like me, she bears the physical scars of that battlefield: the burst blood vessel on my left cheek appeared during labor with Julia. It still spreads spidery-red fingers across my face. The root canal brought on by my pregnancy with Christian left me with a porcelain crown. A seven-inch, maroon scar bisects my lower abdomen. Just below it is another, faded to flesh. Stretch marks ornament my breasts and hips like silver ribbons. My hips are two sizes wider, my feet a size bigger than when I was married—my very bones have expanded in response to my mothering. Some of the effects are temporary, just for the moments of pregnancy: the bleeding gums, the weakened bladder, the hair that falls out in clumps, the intermittent back pain, and aching hips. These pass in their time, but the memory remains.

In that memory lies the glory of this earthly body: though we may be resurrected in a perfect frame, the lessons taught me by my mother-body will rise with me. The sacrifice, the pain, the fear and faith of my mothering will sink into my soul and remain with me in the eternities. My spirit and this woman's body inseparably connected constitute my fullness of joy. Time writes its messages on all of us. Our very bodies have become our book of life. To what have we been obedient? To the purpose for which we were made: to provide a body and a safe haven for the spirits entrusted to our care. If we mother well, we wear out our lives bringing to pass the lives of others. Of the physical fruits—our wider hips, our sagging breasts, our flatter feet, and rounder buttocks—we need not be so ashamed.

Finding the Joy

I AM A MOTHER

Jane Clayson Johnson

A couple of years ago, my husband and I attended a dinner meeting outside Washington, D.C. It was a wonderful gathering of about seventy-five mostly LDS couples from a variety of professions, including law, business, education, and communications. After dinner, each of us was asked to introduce him- or herself.

The men in the room confidently and appropriately stated their professional achievements, which were impressive. They had degrees; they served on boards; they tended to patients and served clients; they had accomplished sons and daughters.

Then their wives stood up—beautiful, intelligent, spiritual women. Many of them had served on boards, held degrees, and were seasoned in their respective fields. Each of them was also a mother.

But this is how many of the women described themselves:

"Oh, I'm just a mom."

"I don't have any credentials; I'm just raising our six children."

"My life's not very exciting right now; I'm just a stay-at-home mom."

"I don't have much to offer here. I'm just a mother."

We heard some variation of the phrase "I'm just a mother" repeated, almost apologetically, over and over again.

Their words surprised me. I had recently given birth to my first child, and I was on top of the world. My baby was a blessing that had come to me a little later in life than usual, and I was excited and honored to finally accept the mantle of motherhood. I felt an extraordinary sense of responsibility. And *power.* Not as the world defines the word, but from entering a sacred partnership with the Creator himself. What a remarkable gift! I wanted to shout from the rooftops, "I am a mother! I am a mother!"

So when I heard these women say, "I'm *just* a mother," I was taken aback. Was I missing something? Did these lovely women—these experienced mothers—know something I didn't? Was it simply a matter of time before I'd figure it out? Before I, too, would understand that motherhood was somehow of lesser importance?

When I left my television career in New York City to get married and to have a family, many of my colleagues told me I was crazy, that I was out of my mind. I had turned down a lucrative, four-year network contract, working on exciting, high-profile, prime-time projects.

Some people were incredibly supportive. One

producer in particular came into my office, looked me straight in the eye, and said, "Good for you!" He wasn't endorsing my decision to be a mother *per se,* but he did congratulate me for having the courage to follow my heart, to act on my convictions.

By way of contrast, when I explained to another rather influential colleague that I would not be taking that contract offer, he told me I was making a terrible decision that I would regret for years to come. "What will you *be* without your job?" he asked. "If you leave television now, you're *done.*"

I found that the reaction from my female colleagues was largely, and disappointingly, less than supportive. I shared my decision with one woman who smugly joked, "Why don't you just get a nanny?" Another network executive asked me what I was going to do once I got to Boston. I told her I was going to have a family, I was going to be a mother. "No, I understand that," she said, puzzled, "but what are you going to *do?*"

All of this was still fresh on my mind during that evening spent near Washington, D.C. A chorus of "I'm *just* a mother," juxtaposed with "What will you be without your job?" and "You're making a terrible mistake" made me wonder, *Could they be right?*

What I have since learned is that *God's* definition of motherhood and the *world's* definition are vastly different. And sometimes—probably all too often—the challenges, daily physical and emotional exhaustion, and occasional self-doubt that come along with being a mother cause many of us to buy into an inaccurate and destructive understanding of our role. There just doesn't seem to be a lot of joy—or fulfillment—associated with the world's interpretation of motherhood.

At times, there may be few immediate rewards for those of us who are mothers. There are no Christmas bonuses, no promotions, no paid vacations. But there is love, there is laughter, there is joy. And there are assurances. For, as the Apostle Paul taught, "Eye hath not seen, nor ear heard, neither have entered into the heart of man, the things which God hath prepared for them that love him" (1 Corinthians 2:9). A mother who loves the Lord and teaches her children to do the same—above all else—cannot be denied this blessing.

What power we would possess if every mother would turn off the voices of the world and instead truly believe what the Lord has promised!

Are you protective of that role? When asked, do you meekly respond that you're "*just* a mother," or do you confidently declare, "I am a mother"?

We must revere motherhood in our homes, in our Church callings, in our places of employment, in our associations with our neighbors, in everything we do. When mothers themselves begin to revere their callings, so much can change. And surely, when a woman of virtue values motherhood above other pursuits, her children will "arise up, and call her blessed" (Proverbs 31:28).

Still, the sanctity of motherhood can be hard to appreciate when you spend endless hours making peanut butter and jelly sandwiches, singing along with Elmo, helping create elaborate science projects, or enforcing late-night curfews. Many in the world will shout that motherhood is full of small, mundane tasks. And certainly, if you look only on the surface, this is true. But underneath all of the secondary things mothers do—cook, clean, read, chauffeur, nurse, and so on—is a mother's real occupation and, I believe, the definition of true success. Webster defines *occupation* as "the principal business of one's life." The principal business of a mother's life is loving and nurturing her children; it is teaching them, by example, how to pass on that love and thereby strengthening the world around them.

I believe, from the depths of my heart, that a righteous mother is the embodiment of success. I believed this about motherhood before I got married and had children. Now, I *know* it: As a woman, the most important work I will ever do will happen within the walls of my own home.

Having said that, I must admit that there are some days when I think it would be easier, if not preferable, to be a foreign correspondent than to be a mother. There are definitely moments when I am down on my hands and knees, mopping up yet another mess, when I look up at the TV to see one of my old friends interviewing someone famous or globe-trotting on a big story, and I think, *What have I done?* But as I look at the little faces of my children, I realize I would not trade in my current occupation. Not for anything.

I know what I gave up so that I could be a mother during this season of my life. But I also know what I gave it up for. I traded in fancy lunches in fancy restaurants for rice cereal and bunny-shaped macaroni and cheese. There's no one to do my hair and makeup anymore. Some mornings I'm lucky to squeeze in a shower. When I get up at 4:00 a.m. these days, it's not to be chauffeured to a television studio. Instead, you'll find me huddled near a nightlight, lulling a little baby (or two!) back to sleep. No more pats on the back for booking exclusive interviews. They don't give awards for best diaper change of the day. And I don't get a paycheck that can be cashed at any bank. Now my compensation comes in packages money can't buy.

Indeed, every mother who prayerfully chooses her own path in life—no matter where that path leads—does not have to apologize for being a mother. As she loves her children, as she sacrifices—in her own way and within her own capabilities—she will be led by the Savior and buoyed up by his loving care as she works to rear "the offspring" of God (Acts 17:28). In this, she will have acquired true success.

Even when our children cannot—or *will not*—express it, even when the voices of the world tell us that mothering isn't as important as anything else we could be doing, *we are making a difference.*

The next time someone inquires what you do or asks you to describe yourself, would you say with confidence and with joy, "I am a mother"?

I never *imagined* that I would have a child that complained every night if we didn't have peanut butter and jelly sandwiches for dinner. I never thought that there would be winters when we never had everyone well at one time and that I wouldn't get an uninterrupted night's sleep for years on end. It never dawned on me that there would be times I would feel overwhelmed, exhausted, and inadequate. But neither did I imagine the *joy* of holding my own baby, the *delight* of listening to a three-year-old's imaginative play, or the *pride* of watching my own kindergartener in a school Christmas play. The expectations of motherhood are not always fulfilled, but often they are *surpassed*.

AMY HARDISON

"GET USED TO IT"

Karen J. Ashton

Moments after my first baby's birth they placed her in my arms. As I touched her tiny fingers I laughed and cried at the same time. She was beautiful! She opened her eyes and looked, for the first time, at the mortal world she was now a part of. I was seeing a brand new world myself. I was looking through the eyes of a mother. The pathway of life ahead of me, which had seemed to contain so many choices moments ago, had suddenly straightened out. Someone else's life and well-being depended on me. There would be no skydiving lessons, speedboat racing, or any other high-risk adventures. I prayed I would be equal to the responsibility. I was determined to be the best mother, homemaker, housekeeper, hostess, Saint, and citizen the world had ever seen.

The windows of heaven opened over the next few years and it rained babies. By the time Emily was three we had two other children and a good case of reality had set in. There were dishes, diapers, earaches, doctors, errands, and meals. That doesn't begin to mention the weightier responsibilities of teaching my little ones the gospel and being a worthy example. Nothing I had ever heard or read had prepared me for the physical and emotional intensity of motherhood. Physically, there was no rest. I had a new sympathy for the little robin outside my window who was forever feeding and warming her young. Emotionally, huge roots of love had grown into and around my heart. I knew that if something were to hurt my children or suddenly take them from me I would bleed uncontrollably. I loved my children as I had never loved anything or anyone in my life. Even when I managed to get away, the anxiety for their well-being would thunder over me like a herd of elephants. Frankly, I was exhausted.

One morning, I called my mother and cried: "I'm so tired. I'm going to die!" Her reply was short and to the point. "Get used to it. You're going to feel that way the rest of your life." I was stunned by her blunt and seemingly uncaring remark. Later that day I happened to relate my mother's comment to another young mother. I couldn't believe it. She laughed! Then, to my surprise, I laughed too. Neither of us questioned the truth of what my mother had said. Somehow, laughing about it brought relief and broke the tension and fatigue I had been feeling all morning.

Because parenthood is the highest and holiest of callings, it's easy to feel overwhelmed with the responsibility and forget to enjoy the process. The Lord wants us to be happy and find joy in our work as well as joy in our posterity. Understanding God's love for us and for our children should fill us with hope, happiness, and good cheer.

A DENTED MINIVAN

Lisa Valentine Clark

I sometimes forget that the make, model, and condition of my car does not indicate who I am—who I *really* am. Well, that's not entirely true. I actually love the dent on the driver's side of the minivan because it reminds me of how much I live on the edge.

One 24th of July we were visiting some friends when their neighbors brought over some serious fireworks. As we "oooed!" and "ahhhhed!," all looking straight up in the air, mouths agape, unbeknownst to us, the firework package had tipped over and was pointed straight at us all. A neighbor ran to tip the firework back into its upright position just in time for the next round to go off and run up his cheek, dangerously near his eye. We saw him place the package upright on the ground, then watched it knock itself over again and shoot the next round right across the street, into my van door. I love that dent. It means the children are safe and we made a good story together. Later that evening, the neighbor brought over custom lemon custard as we all retold his feat of "*literally* saving our lives and risking his eye" in the process, and

143

we imagined in detail, with "tsks!" and "wows!," what would have happened if the fireworks had shot into the crowd: we exclaimed in excited tones and moved our heads side to side. Yes, a hero and a family tale were born that night. And the dent remains.

My minivan is also a litmus test in problem solving, so I feel like I'm really giving my kids an advantage for the future in that regard. It amazes me that most kids today truly don't know how to open up a van door. This happens 100 percent of the time anyone under the age of twenty-one comes into my 2000 Dodge Grand Caravan: They stand in front of the door, waiting for it to open automatically. It doesn't. This car was built before most of them were born. I yell, "You have to open the door! It's not one of those that open . . . you're just going to have to slide it . . . yank it open!" At this point they look confused and inevitably shrug, presumably looking for a doorknob/handle/lever, and about 23 percent of them locate it, but of those 23 percent, none of them can successfully operate it to open the door. Not one. It's the weirdest phenomenon. They yank. They look confused, and, preemptively, while my own kids have been staring at the door or looking aimlessly around at no one in particular, I've been telling them, "Just do it. Just open the door. Just . . ." and soon my kids are telling their friends (like it's obvious), "JUST PUSH THE BUTTON AND SLIDE THE DOOR OPEN!" Twelve percent of that group is able to, and I usually sigh at this point. (My youngest, Margaret, always asks me why I sigh so loud. I tell her I'm just trying to catch my breath. Which I am. I'm also reevaluating the choices that brought me to this point. This "point of SIGH.")

Ultimately, they either yank the handle to the side and the door opens (5 percent of the time) or one of my kids opens it. And that's what technology is doing to our kids: They can't OPEN DOORS, PEOPLE! And then, 98 percent of the time, my kids say something like "When are we getting a new car?" and I catch my breath. Really loudly.

It's not like I don't dream of or imagine better cars, a better home, a more glamorous life. But I've made my choices. And I own them. Of course, that's easy to say when things are running relatively smoothly. When your kids are all snug in their beds dreaming away, the kitchen is clean, the floors are clear of dirty socks and random bits of paper, and all you can hear is the gentle hum of the dishwasher, it's easy to be satisfied that everything's all right and you're on top of it all. It's when you find your basement flooding, or discover your kid isn't turning in school assignments, or realize you've missed a work deadline—that's when you begin to worry that everything is falling apart, or could at a moment's notice, like that critical block in the middle of the Jenga game that brings everything crashing down.

It is often said that motherhood is a lot of things: a roller coaster, a bad boyfriend, a carnival, a marathon, a horror movie, whatever, but really motherhood is unlike anything else. And I'm not even trying to say that it's like a dented minivan (although if this were a question on the ACT, minivans to mothers is like space shuttle to astronaut) because that comparison doesn't fully capture it all either. I mean, I like the analogy in the sense that we're on a journey together, there's room for everyone, and it's messy but fun. But the van metaphor for motherhood could go the other way, too: it's just to get from point A to point B, it breaks down a lot, it depreciates in value (see, not a great comparison—pretty flawed, actually).

Motherhood defies analogy and categorization because as prepared as we think we are, as motivated, well-intentioned, and dedicated, we never seem to be the kind of mother we set out to be. That can be both good and bad. Motherhood changes us. It has us constantly adjusting for the unexpected. And it has a way of revealing the best and worst in us, which is a beautiful, humiliating way of life. Living on the edge.

Protective mother love is the guardian of youth, but protection too long continued makes for weakness, not strength, in the child. To watch the tiny, helpless infant grow and develop under your constant, watchful care is to see a miracle wrought. To live again in the enthusiasm and activity of youth with your children is to intensify and enrich life's drama. To be *counselor* and *protector*, knowing when to assist and when to recede into the background, that your child may learn to walk alone, calls for almost superhuman wisdom. Wise indeed is the mother who has found the source of divine aid through prayer and who begins with the little child at her knee, teaching that child to pray to our all-wise Heavenly Father for the *strength* that will protect him or her against the forces of evil. A true mother's objective is to teach and train wisely until she can say with assurance, "My children are strong enough to walk alone with faith as their guide."

CAMILLA EYRING KIMBALL

CAN I BE A JOYFUL MOTHER?

Linda J. Eyre

Although it's no fun to be buried in a trial, those mothers who have passed through them also believe that their trials were great teachers. There may be months or even years when these mothers have struggled to find joy in their lives. Their trials gave them hard times that they never would have asked for. Yet, satisfaction comes from knowing that what they learned in the process is one of their most precious possessions. If we have faith that what we are learning is part of God's plan for us, no matter how hard it seems at the time, we can feel a sort of calmness through our tribulations while trying our best to come up with solutions to our problems.

The answer, I believe, to "Can I be joyful despite all my trials and tribulations?" is "Yes!" Not every day or even every season, not in every way or without sometimes wishing life was different, but in your heart of hearts, you *can* know that part of the process of feeling joy is working through your tribulations. If we put the happiness of our lives in God's hands and have faith that we are here to learn from adversity, everything can become a process of feeling joy and its many aspects.

CHOOSING MOTHERHOOD AGAIN

Janene W. Baadsgaard

Motherhood is not for wimps. When you're pregnant, your body turns into a science fair project—only you're not in charge of the hypothesis, experiment, or outcome. After the baby gets here, you're sucked on, pooped on, spit on, chewed on, and wet on. Then later you get kicked, punched, screamed at, disobeyed, and run away from. You eat cold meals, wear stained clothes, and never get enough sleep. When your children are finally old enough to help, they won't. When your children are teenagers and their friends come over, they ask you to hide in your bedroom and not come out until their friends leave. When they move away from home for college, they only call home when they want something.

So why in the world do we do it? We do it because if we didn't, children would die or never be born. Society would cease to exist. The world as we know it would come to an end. I know of no other life work that can make that claim.

Those who do the most good in this world are often largely

invisible and receive the least credit or payment. When governments, financial institutions, and nations fail, mothers offer the answers—brand new people wrapped in flannel. We give the world fresh human beings with novel ideas, unique talents, and visionary answers to age-old problems. And we do it because we have chosen *not* to put ourselves first. We have chosen to be the stewards of a new generation. We have chosen to be the moral earth where the rising generation's roots can sink deep in time-honored values. We have chosen to offer our unconditional love, our time, our talents, and everything we have so that our children can grow up with a smile in the audience, forgiving arms in a crisis, and a push of encouragement at the door when they leave the nest and learn to fly.

No community or nation will survive without us. We feed the hungry, clothe the naked, and house the homeless. It doesn't matter if anyone else, including our own spouse and children, appreciates us if *we* do. When we catch a glimpse of what it means to be a mother and how our actions or failure to act will affect thousands for generations, we will never undervalue our contribution again.

Motherhood frees us to love someone more than ourselves and gives a dimension of sacredness to everything we do. Motherhood liberates us from selfishness and creates a gentler world where someone is always looking out for others.

Motherhood releases us from a life of get and introduces us to a life of give.

With the years and years of nurturing, feeding, hugging, reading, and cleaning, we are granted the ability to love and the opportunity to be loved. Our hearts open to the value of another human being in ways we didn't before comprehend. We are transformed as we transcend self.

So on those hard days, choose motherhood *again* with even greater tenderness and commitment. I absolutely promise you that every sacrifice you make for your child will contain your life's greatest meaning—every choice to love, your life's greatest purpose.

SOURCES

Books courtesy of Deseret Book Company except where noted.

Anonymous birth mother, in Elaine Cannon, *Mothering* (Bookcraft, 1993).

Ashton, Karen J., in Barbara B. Smith and Shirley W. Thomas, eds., *Behold Your Little Ones* (Bookcraft, 1999).

Baadsgaard, Janene W., *For Every Mother* (Covenant Communications, 2011).

Bennion, Francine R., in Smith and Thomas, eds., *Behold Your Little Ones.*

Campbell, Beverly, *Eve and the Choice Made in Eden* (Bookcraft, 2003).

Cannon, Elaine, *Mothering* (Bookcraft, 1993).

Choules, Marilyn Jeppson, in Smith and Thomas, *Behold Your Little Ones.*

Clark, Lisa Valentine, *Real Moms: Making It Up as We Go* (2015).

Cook, Mary N., "Animal Pancakes: How Making Breakfast Brought Me into the Cook Tent," Time Out for Women blog post, November 18, 2015.

Dalton, Elaine S., *No Ordinary Women* (2016).

Day, Afton, *How to Be a Perfect Wife and Other Myths* (Bookcraft, 1977).

Day, Laurel C., "Receiving His Unspeakable Gift," Time Out for Women presentation, 2016.

Dew, Sheri, *Are We Not All Mothers?* (2011).

Edmunds, Mary Ellen, "It's About Time," BYU Women's Conference, 1997.

Edwards, Jaroldeen, *Things I Wish I'd Known Sooner* (1991).

Evans, Joy F., in Smith and Thomas, *Behold Your Little Ones.*

Eyre, Linda J., *A Joyful Mother of Children* (Bookcraft, 1992).

Freeman, Emily Belle, *Even This* (2017).

Hardison, Amy, *How to Feel Great about Being a Mother* (1987).

Harrison, Beppie, *Needles in the Basket* (1991).

Heuston, Kimberley Burton, *Single Parenting* (1998).

Holland, Patricia T., *Strength and Stillness* (2015).

Inouye, Melissa Wei-Tsing, *Crossings* (A Living Faith Book/ BYU Maxwell Institute/ Deseret Book, 2019).

Jensen, Virginia U., "I Can Do All Things through Christ," BYU Women's Conference, 1998.

Johnson, Jane Clayson, *I Am a Mother* (2007).

Kapp, Ardeth G., *My Neighbor, My Sister, My Friend* (1990).

Kimball, Camilla Eyring, in Edward L. Kimball, ed., *The Writings of Camilla Eyring Kimball* (1988).

Lay, KaRyn, "I Didn't Want to Like Her: The Prompting That Helped Me Connect with My Stepkids' Mom," Time Out for Women blog post, May 4, 2017.

Linford, Marilynne Todd, *Is Anyone Out There Building Mother's Self-Esteem?* (1986).

Marriott, Neill, *Seek This Jesus* (2017).

McCann, Mary Holland, *In Mary's Arms* (2016).

Nadauld, Margaret D., "Like a Lioness at the Gates of the Home," BYU Women's Conference, 2011.

Null, Kathleen "Casey," *Where Are We Going Besides Crazy?* (Bookcraft, 1989).

Okazaki, Chieko, *Shared Motherhood* (Bookcraft, 1994).

Olson, Camille Fronk, *Mary, the Mother of Jesus* (2012).

Pearce, Virginia H., *Where Heaven Meets You* (2016).

Permann, Whitney, "You Are Their Perfect Mother," Time Out for Women blog post, November 8, 2015.

Rasmus, Carolyn, in *In His Hands* (2015).

Reed, Calee, "I Know Where Your Mommy Is—She's with My Mommy," Time Out for Women blog post, April 27, 2018.

Reeves, Linda S., "The Vital Role of Women in the Gospel," BYU Women's Conference, 2012.

Romney, Brooke, "Why we are taking the fun out of life," *Deseret News*, June 24, 2015.

Santiago, Tessa Meyer, "'Get Thee Behind Me,'" BYU Women's Conference, 1998.

Schmidt, Michelle, *Carried* (2018).

Smith, Barbara B. and Shirley W. Thomas, *Women of Devotion* (Bookcraft, 1990).

Stone, Breaunna, "When God puts you in the standby line," *Deseret News*, November 16, 2016.

Ulrich, Wendy, *Live Up to Our Privileges* (2019).

Vranes, Zandra, Sistas in Zion social media post, July 8, 2019.

Walker, Kathleen H., in Virginia H. Pearce, ed., *Glimpses into the Life and Heart of Marjorie Pay Hinckley* (1988).

Watts, Emily, *The Slow-Ripening Fruits of Mothering* (2013).

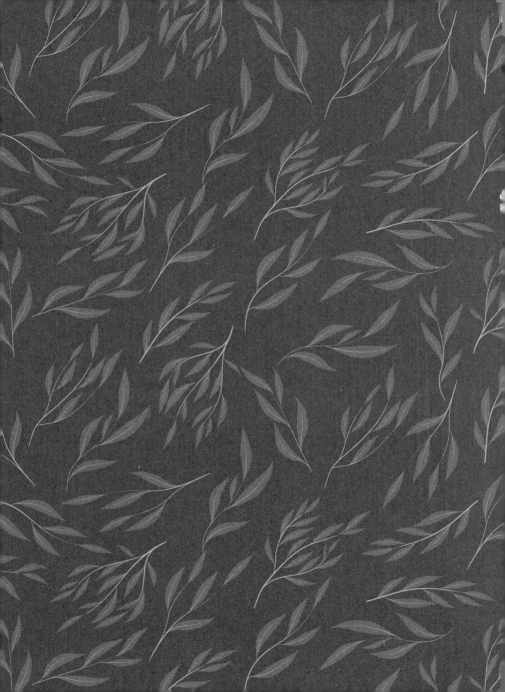